Timber Resource Statistics For Western Oregon, 1997

David L. Azuma, Larry F. Bednar,
Bruce A. Hiserote, and
Charles F. Veneklase

Resource Bulletin
PNW-RB-237
October 2004
REVISED

 United States
Department of
Agriculture

 Forest
Service

 Pacific Northwest
Research Station

Authors

David L. Azuma is a research forester, **Larry F. Bednar** was a mathematical statistician, **Bruce A. Hiserote** is a forester, and **Charles F. Veneklase** is a computer specialist, Forestry Sciences Laboratory, P.O. Box 3890, Portland, OR 97208-3890. Bednar is now a consultant, Portland, OR.

Abstract

Azuma, David L.; Bednar, Larry F.; Hiserote, Bruce A.; Veneklase, Charles F. 2004. Timber resource statistics for western Oregon, 1997. Rev. Resour. Bull. PNW-RB-237. Portland, OR: U.S. Department of Agriculture, Forest Service, Pacific Northwest Research Station. 120 p.

This report is a summary of timber resource statistics for western Oregon, which includes Benton, Clackamas, Clatsop, Columbia, Coos, Curry, Douglas, Hood River, Jackson, Josephine, Lane, Lincoln, Linn, Marion, Multnomah, Polk, Tillamook, Washington, and Yamhill Counties. Data were collected as part of a statewide multiresource inventory. The inventory sampled all private and public lands except those administered by the National Forest System and the Bureau of Land Management (BLM). The National Forest System and BLM provided data from regional inventories. Area information for parks and other reserves was obtained directly from the organizations managing these areas. Statistical tables provide estimates of land area, timber volume, growth, mortality, and harvest for individual survey units and at the half-state level.

Keywords: Forest surveys, forest inventory, statistics (forest), timber resources, resources (forest), western Oregon.

Summary

Western Oregon has an estimated 19 million acres of land. About 80 percent of this land is forested with 71 percent being timberland. Lands administered by the U.S. Department of Agriculture, Forest Service, National Forest System (NFS) and U.S. Department of the Interior, Bureau of Land Management (BLM) make up about 48 percent of the timberland. Within the nonfederal timberland area, net volume of growing stock is estimated as 23.5 billion cubic feet. About 58 percent of the volume is administered by forest industry, 20 percent by other public owners, and 21 percent by other private owners. About 82 percent of the total growing stock volume is in coniferous species, with Douglas-fir accounting for 74 percent of the conifer volume. Estimated net annual growth of growing stock for nonfederal lands is 0.77 billion cubic feet, and average annual mortality for this timber is an estimated 0.1 billion cubic feet.

Preface

Forest Inventory and Analysis (FIA) is a nationwide program of the USDA Forest Service authorized by the Forest and Rangeland Renewable Resources Research Act of 1978. Work units at Forest Service research and experiment stations conduct forest resource inventories throughout the 50 states. The FIA Program of the Pacific Northwest Research Station in Portland, Oregon, is responsible for forest inventories in Alaska, California, Hawaii, Oregon, and Washington.

Contents

List of Tables

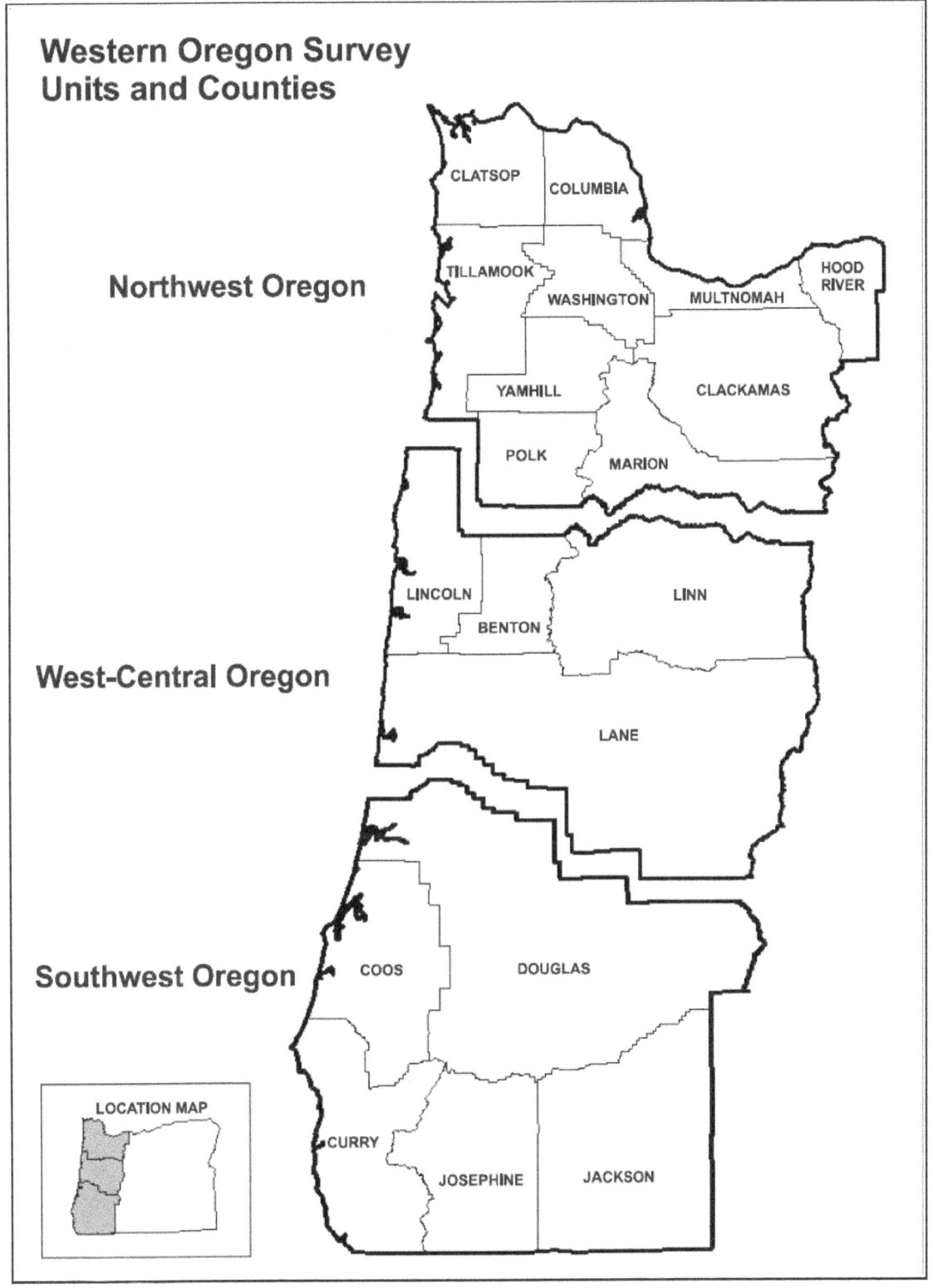

Western Oregon Survey
Units and Counties

Northwest Oregon

CLATSOP
COLUMBIA
TILLAMOOK
WASHINGTON
MULTNOMAH
HOOD RIVER
YAMHILL
CLACKAMAS
POLK
MARION

West-Central Oregon

LINCOLN
LINN
BENTON
LANE

Southwest Oregon

COOS
DOUGLAS
CURRY
JOSEPHINE
JACKSON

LOCATION MAP

Introduction

The Forest Inventory and Analysis (FIA) unit of the USDA Forest Service, Pacific Northwest Research Station conducted a multiresource inventory in western Oregon's forests between 1994 and 1998. This inventory included all lands except those administered by the Forest Service and the U.S. Department of the Interior, Bureau of Land Management (BLM). This report summarizes the timber resource statistics for western Oregon's forests. Some statistical tables include inventory data provided by the Forest Service and the BLM for area on their lands. Other resources sampled but not included in this report are understory vegetation, crown cover, coarse woody debris, and snags. These data will lead to further analysis of the status of western Oregon's forests.

This FIA unit has been reporting statistics for western Oregon since the 1930s. Hazard and Metcalf (1964, 1965), Metcalf and Hazard (1964), Bassett (1977), Jacobs (1978), Mei (1979), and Gedney and others (1986a, 1986b, 1987) reported inventory statistics in the 1960s, 1970s, and 1980s. The current grid system was a systematic sample implemented in the early 1960s; before this grid, a type map system was used for inventory statistics. McKay and others (1998) used an updated 1994 data set to report the latest forest statistics for western Oregon.

This report contains statistical tables that provide current estimates of forest land area, change estimates for nonfederal lands, number of trees, timber volume, growth, mortality, and harvest. In several tables, area data supplied to the 1997 Resources Planning Act (RPA) by the National Forest System are incorporated. The national forest statistics include areas that are withdrawn from full production but still meet the FIA definition of timberland. National forest lands are not equally available for timber production because management must consider policies such as the Northwest Forest Plan and riparian reserves in decisionmaking.

Highlights

About 80 percent of western Oregon's land is forested with about 71 percent being timberland. Federal agencies—the National Forest System and the Bureau of Land Management—administer about 48 percent of the timberland. Owners classed as forest industry administer about 31 percent of the timberland; nonindustrial and other public owners administer about 13 and 6 percent of timberland, respectively.

The production of timber has shifted away from federal lands to state and privately owned lands. In the 1980s, federal lands produced an average of 2.66 billion board feet per year. In the 1990s, that number dropped to 0.79 billion board feet per year, with a 0.19 billion average between 1995 and 1997. Other public and private lands averaged 3.0 billion board feet in the 1980s and decreased 5 percent to 2.85 billion in the 1990s. The 70-percent reduction from federal lands does not represent a change in land class, but is evidence of changing availability of land for timber production based on new management decisions. Federal land areas with reduced availability include, but are not limited to, riparian reserves, wildlife reserves, and access-limited areas.

The stand size for nonfederal owners in western Oregon tends to be skewed to the small size classes. About 5 percent of the nonfederal lands have an average stand diameter of 21 inches or greater, and 43 percent have an average stand diameter between 5 and 11 inches. Public owners such as state, county, and other federal owners have about 10 percent of their lands with an average diameter of 21 inches or greater. Forest industry and nonindustrial private owners have about 4 percent of their land in the larger diameters. Forty-eight percent of all nonfederal lands have stand diameters between 11 and 21 inches.

Nonfederal timberlands in western Oregon show an increase in standing volume from 20.1 to 23.3 billion cubic feet based on plots measured during the previous and present inventories. Growth is 33 percent greater than removals plus mortality for nonfederal lands in western Oregon. The growth greater than removals plus mortality differs by survey unit with the southwest unit having the lowest percentage at 16 percent, followed by the west-central unit at 21 percent, and the northwest unit at 63 percent.

A minor net loss of timberland—51,000 of 6.9 million acres—is due to land use change. Most of the losses in timberland came from previous timberland being reclassed as roads. The 189,000-acre loss in timberland to urban, agriculture, and other nonforest uses is offset by the 138,000-acre gain from nonforest and other forest becoming timberland. Reclassification of lands from the previous inventory accounts for an additional 184,000 acres of timberland.

Inventory Procedures (Nonfederal Lands)

Western Oregon was inventoried by using a double sampling for stratification scheme (Cochran 1977). The sampling is implemented on a permanent systematic grid and produces an even geographic distribution of both secondary (field) and primary (photo) plots across the state. Photo plots are placed at random inside each square of the grid.

The primary sample for western Oregon consists of a grid of about 24,000 points established in 1994 by using aerial photographs taken in 1994. Data collected on each point included amount of tree cover by species group, average conifer height, disturbance codes, owner, and stage of development.

The secondary sample consisted of 1,478 forest and nonforest field locations established in previous inventories and remeasured or reclassified in the 1994-98 period. This sample represents about a 1-in-16 subsample of the primary sample. The ratio of 1 field to 16 photo plots provides a sufficient number of plots to meet the required sampling precision for estimates of forest area and volume.

The national forest and BLM plots were based on a similar grid system with a different plot design (Max and others 1996). The data were collected for these inventories between 1993 and 1996 and are in the 1997 RPA database.

In 1984-86 a cluster of five subplots was installed at timberland grid locations. At that time, the subplots sampled a single homogeneous condition, by moving subplots into the condition if necessary. Variable-radius sampling was used to select trees over 5 inches diameter at breast height (d.b.h.), and a smaller fixed-radius plot was used to sample seedlings and saplings.

In 1994, the sampling design was modified to remove potential bias inherent in the 1984-86 procedures. The term "condition class" was defined for the modified design to identify different situations that could occur on a plot. A condition class, or "condition," refers to an area with a distinct land class (timberland, woodland, nonforest, etc.) and vegetative condition (forest type, stand age, etc.). The modified design requires that the field plots maintain fixed locations for all subplots in the cluster. Plots that straddle two or more conditions sample all conditions by establishing each subplot in the designated position and mapping the boundaries around each condition. The information pertinent to each condition is recorded as condition-class attributes. When multiple conditions exist on a plot, all data in one condition are processed together. This can impact the amount of information present to classify stand characteristics such as forest type, stand size, and stand age. On 1,478 field plots in the 1995-97 inventory, 2,754 condition classes were sampled, of which 1,403 were timberland conditions. Roads accounted for most nonforest conditions existing on plots.

Land and Water Area Updated

The U.S. Department of Commerce, Bureau of the Census compiles and publishes the acreage of land and water in the United States every 10 years. These area figures, available by state and county, are accepted and used by FIA in Portland, Oregon, as the gross number of acres to be inventoried in each county. The previous inventory was based on 1980 census data, and the current inventory uses 1990 census figures. Raster-scanned topographic maps from the U.S. Department of the Interior, Geological Survey and a geographic information system are now used by the Bureau of the Census to identify water bodies and landforms and to determine the size of much smaller areas than previously possible. As a result, the definition of inland water was changed to reflect the finer resolution. Streams with a minimum width of 200 feet are now recognized, compared to 660 feet in 1980; small water bodies are now at least 4.5 acres, compared to 40 acres in the past.

Change in Ownership Definitions

Land owned by Native Americans is now classified as "other private." In the 1986-87 inventory, these lands were defined as "other public." Forest industry was divided into the two categories of "forest industry with mills" and "forest industry without mills"; both are now classed as "forest industry."

Analysis of Change Between Inventories for Nonfederal Lands

To analyze change in forest statistics, the 1986-87 data were recompiled to account for technical changes in the 1995-97 inventory. The summaries presented in tables 27a through 29d have been developed from remeasured plots outside of federal lands and include recompiled data from the 1986-87 inventory. Caution should be used in comparing present statistics and those published by Gedney and others (1986a, 1986b, 1987) because of procedural changes, stratification differences, and plot changes. Comparing estimates from previous to current ones is like comparing independent estimates of the resource at different points in time; although both are valid estimates, they will not be equal.

Reliability of Inventory Data

Inventories conducted by FIA are designed to provide sampling errors consistent with national standards set by the Forest Service. The target error for total timberland area is 3 percent per million acres and 10 percent per billion cubic feet of growing-stock volume.

The sample design for this inventory provides the highest precision when estimates are aggregated for an entire survey unit such as the northwest, west-central, or southwest units in western Oregon. As the sample is divided into smaller units, the confidence intervals increase in relation to the size of the estimate. Confidence intervals are quantitative expressions of the variability inherent in the estimation procedures for area and volume. The tabulation below indicates, for instance, a 68-percent (one standard error) chance that the true timberland area for nonfederal owners in the northwest unit (2,369,000 acres) is within the range of 2,322,000 to 2,416,000 acres.

Standard errors for nonfederal timberland area, by owner class and survey unit, are displayed below:

Survey unit	Other public	Forest industry	Other private	All owners
		Thousand acres (± standard error)		
Northwest	574±40	1,103±50	692±48	2,369±47
West-central	98±26	1,339±47	431±42	1,867±38
Southwest	179±32	1,736±55	759±48	2,809±48

Standard errors for growing-stock volume on nonfederal timberland area, by owner class and survey unit, are displayed below:

Survey unit	Other public	Forest industry	Other private	All owners
	Million cubic feet (± standard error)			
Northwest	3,075±279	4,514±355	2,194±218	9,783±400
West- central	411±116	4,382±307	1,400±174	6,194±334
Southwest	900±182	4,625±301	2,014±185	7,538±348

Confidence intervals vary with the size of the estimate and the amount of variance associated with the estimate. The following is a set of approximate confidence intervals calculated by using a regression analysis between actual standard error and the estimate involved. These regressions have r-square values greater than 0.86, indicating that 86 percent of the variance in the relation can be explained by the equation. The actual error estimates for cells in tables can be obtained from the Portland FIA unit.

Timberland area			Growing-stock volume		
Estimate	Interval	Percent	Estimate	Interval	Percent
Thousand acres			Million cubic feet		
3,000	±126	4	6,000	±240	4
2,000	±89	4	4,000	±173	4
1,500	±66	4	2,000	±143	7
1,000	±54	5	1,000	±104	10
800	±48	6	800	±94	12
600	±42	7	600	±83	14
400	±34	8	400	±70	18
200	±25	12	200	±52	26
100	±18	18	100	±40	40
50	±13	26	50	±31	62
25	±10	40	25	±25	99
15	±8	53			
10	±6	60			
5	±5	99			

Terminology

Available other forest land—Forest land incapable of growing 20 cubic feet per acre per year (mean annual increment at culmination in fully stocked, natural stands) of industrial wood because of adverse conditions such as sterile soils, dry climate, poor drainage, subalpine sites, steepness, or rockiness.

Bureau of Land Management land—Land administered by the U.S. Department of the Interior, Bureau of Land Management.

Class of timber—A classification of trees as growing stock, cull, and salvable dead. Growing-stock trees are divided into poletimber and sawtimber trees.

Condition class—A mapped area on a plot with a distinct land class (for example, timberland, oak woodland, nonforest) or a distinct vegetative condition (for example, forest type, stand size). The first condition identified at plot center is the only condition that is remeasured and used for the analysis of periodic change.

County and municipal lands—Lands owned by county and other local public agencies.

Cull trees—Live trees of noncommercial species and live trees of commercial species that are more than 75-percent defective. Noncommercial species are apple, black locust, holly, junipers, Pacific yew, Pacific dogwood, white alder, and willow. Cull trees are not growing-stock trees.

Cull trees, rotten—Cull trees with defect caused primarily by rot.

Cull trees, sound—Trees of noncommercial species or cull trees of commercial species with defect caused primarily by poor form and roughness.

Diameter class—A classification of trees based on diameter outside the bark measured at breast height, 4½ feet above the ground. The common abbreviation for diameter at breast height is d.b.h. Trees are grouped into 2-inch classes up to 21 inches d.b.h., after which the class intervals become broader.

Even-aged stands—Stands where 70 percent or more of the tree stocking falls within three adjacent 10-year age classes.

Farmer-owned lands—Lands owned by the operators of farms.

Forest industry lands—Lands owned by companies that grow timber for industrial use. Includes companies both with and without wood processing plants.

Forest land—Land at least 10 percent stocked with live trees, or land that had this minimum tree stocking in the past and is not currently developed for nonforest use. The minimum area recognized is 1 acre; it must be 115 feet wide.

Forest types—Stands are assigned a pure softwood, pure hardwood, softwood-hardwood mix, or hardwood-softwood forest type. Stands with 70 percent or more of the stocking in live softwood trees are classified as pure softwood types and are assigned the type name of the softwood species with the greatest stocking among all softwoods on the condition class plot. Stands with 70 percent or more of the stocking in live hardwood trees are classified as pure hardwood types and are assigned the type name of the hardwood species with the greatest stocking among all hardwoods on the condition class plot. Mixed species types are assigned if softwood stocking is 31 to 69 percent total stocking on the plot; stands with 50 to 69 percent of the stocking in live softwood trees are classed as softwood-hardwood types and receive a type name that includes the softwood species with the greatest softwood stocking, followed by the hardwood species with the greatest hardwood stocking; stands with 51 to 69 percent of the stocking in live hardwood trees are classed as hardwood-softwood types and receive a type name that includes the hardwood species with the greatest hardwood stocking, followed by the softwood species with the greatest softwood stocking. For ease in reporting, the secondary forest type will be identified after a slash as "softwood" or "hardwood" in the summary tables

Growing-stock trees—All live trees growing on timberland except cull trees (see "cull trees").

Growing-stock volume—Net volume in cubic feet of live sawtimber and poletimber growing-stock trees from the top of a stump 12 inches tall to a minimum 4-inch top (of central stem) inside the bark. Net volume is gross volume less deductions for rot and missing bole sections.

Growth, current net annual, growing stock—The increase in growing-stock volume on timberland during the last year of the period between the previous and current inventories. Components of current net annual growth for growing-stock volume include (a) the increment in net volume of poletimber and sawtimber growing-stock trees alive at the beginning of the year and surviving to year end; plus (b) ingrowth, the net volume of growing-stock trees reaching poletimber or sawtimber size during the year; minus (c) mortality, the net volume of poletimber and sawtimber growing-stock trees that died during the year.

Growth, current net annual, sawtimber—The increase in sawtimber volume on timberland during the last year of the period between the previous and current inventories. Components of current net annual growth for sawtimber volume include (a) the increment in net volume of sawtimber trees alive at the beginning of the year and surviving to year end; plus (b) ingrowth, the net volume of trees reaching sawtimber size during the year; minus (c) mortality, the net volume of sawtimber trees that died during the year.

Growth, periodic gross, growing stock—The increase in growing-stock volume between the previous and current inventories that is attributable to increasing tree size. Periodic gross growth includes (a) the increment in net volume of poletimber and sawtimber growing-stock trees alive at both the previous and current inventories; (b) the increment in net volume of poletimber and sawtimber growing-stock trees alive at the previous inventory and harvested between inventories; and (c) ingrowth, the net volume of growing-stock trees reaching poletimber or sawtimber size between inventories.

Growth, periodic gross, sawtimber—The increase in sawtimber volume between the previous and current inventories that is attributable to increasing tree size. Periodic gross growth includes (a) the increment in net volume of sawtimber trees alive at both the previous and current inventories; (b) the increment in net volume of sawtimber trees alive at the previous inventory and harvested between inventories; and (c) ingrowth, the net volume of trees reaching sawtimber size between inventories.

Hardwoods—Nonconiferous trees, usually broad-leaved. See "Names of Trees" for a list of hardwood species in this report.

Industrial wood—All commercial roundwood products except fuelwood. Roundwood includes logs or bolts that are in straight sections at least 8 feet long for hardwoods and 12 feet long for softwoods.

Land area—Area reported as land by the Bureau of the Census (U.S. Department of Commerce 1990). Total land area includes dry land and land temporarily or partially covered by water, such as marshes, swamps, and river flood plains; streams, sloughs, and canals less than 200 feet wide; and lakes, reservoirs, and ponds less than 4.5 acres in area.

Land class—A classification of land by major use. The minimum area for classification is 1 acre.

Mean annual increment (MAI) at culmination—A measure of the productivity of forest land expressed as the average increase in cubic-foot volume per acre per year. For a given species and site index, the mean is based on the age at which the mean annual increment culminates for fully stocked natural stands. The MAI is calculated from equations and is based on the site index of the plot.

Mortality, average annual, growing stock—The annual net volume of poletimber and sawtimber growing-stock trees that died between the previous and current inventories.

Mortality, average annual, sawtimber—The annual net volume of sawtimber trees that died between the previous and current inventories.

National forest lands—Federal lands that have been designated by Executive Order or statute as national forest or purchase units and other lands under the administration of the U.S. Department of Agriculture, Forest Service, including experimental areas and Bankhead-Jones Title III lands.

Native American lands—Tribal and allotted lands held in trust by the federal government. Native American lands are grouped with farmer and miscellaneous private lands as other private lands.

Net volume—Gross volume less deductions for sound and rotten defects. Growing-stock net volume is gross cubic-foot volume less deductions for rot and missing bole sections on poletimber and sawtimber growing-stock trees. Sawtimber net volume is gross board-foot volume less deductions for rot, sweep, crook, missing bole sections, and other defects that affect the use of sawtimber trees for lumber.

Noncommercial species—A tree species not suitable for industrial wood products: apple, black locust, holly, junipers, Pacific yew, Pacific dogwood, white alder, and willow. Noncommercial species will not be included in growing-stock volume tables; however, if one or more of these species dominate on a plot, the forest type might be classified as a noncommercial species.

Nonforest land—Land that has never supported forests or formerly was forested and currently is developed for nonforest uses. Included are lands used for agricultural crops, Christmas tree farms, cottonwood plantations, improved pasture, residential areas, city parks, constructed roads, operating railroads and their right-of-way clearings, powerline and pipeline clearings, streams more than 30 feet wide, and 1- to 40-acre areas of water classified by the U.S. Department of Commerce, Bureau of the Census, as land. If intermingled in forest areas, unimproved roads and other nonforest strips must be more than 120 feet wide, and clearings or other areas must be 1 acre or larger to qualify as nonforest land.

Nonstocked areas—Timberland less than 10 percent stocked with live trees. Recent clearcuts scheduled for planting are classified as nonstocked area.

Other private lands—Private lands not owned by forest industry. Native American lands, farmer-owned lands, and miscellaneous private lands are included.

Other public lands—Lands administered by public agencies other than the U.S. Department of Agriculture, Forest Service and U.S. Department of the Interior, Bureau of Land Management. Other public lands do not include Native American lands, which are included with other private lands.

Poletimber stands—Stands with a quadratic mean diameter (mean diameter weighted by basal area) from 5.0 to 9.0 inches at breast height if a softwood stand and from 5.0 to 11.0 inches at breast height if a hardwood stand.

Poletimber trees—Live growing-stock trees of commercial species that are 5.0 inches in d.b.h. or larger but smaller than sawtimber trees.

Reserved other forest—Forest land incapable of growing 20 cubic feet per acre per year (mean annual increment at culmination in fully stocked, natural stands) of industrial wood that has been dedicated to noncommodity use through statute, ordinance, or administrative order.

Reserved timberland—Forest land capable of growing 20 cubic feet or more per acre per year (mean annual increment at culmination in fully stocked, natural stands) of industrial wood that has been dedicated to noncommodity use through statute, ordinance, or administrative order.

Roundwood—Logs, bolts, or other round sections cut from trees.

Sapling and seedling stands—Stands with a quadratic mean diameter (mean diameter weighted by basal area) less than 5.0 inches at breast height.

Sapling and seedling trees—Live trees of commercial species that are less than 5.0 inches d.b.h. and have no diseases, defects, or deformities likely to prevent their becoming poletimber trees.

Saw-log portion—The bole of sawtimber trees between the stump and the saw-log top. Saw-log top is 7.0 inches in diameter outside bark on softwoods and 9.0 inches in diameter outside bark on hardwoods.

Sawtimber stands—Stands with a quadratic mean diameter (mean diameter weighted by basal area) larger than 9.0 inches at breast height if a softwood stand and larger than 11.0 inches at breast height if a hardwood stand. Small sawtimber stands are sawtimber stands with a mean diameter (weighted by basal area) less than 21.0 inches at breast height. Large sawtimber stands are sawtimber stands that have a mean diameter 21.0 inches or larger at breast height.

Sawtimber trees—Live softwood trees of commercial species at least 9.0 inches d.b.h. and live hardwood trees of commercial species at least 11.0 inches d.b.h. At least 25 percent of the board-foot volume in a sawtimber tree must be free from defect. Softwood trees must contain at least one 12-foot saw log with a top diameter of not less than 7 inches outside bark; hardwood trees must contain at least one 8-foot saw log with a top diameter of not less than 9 inches outside bark.

Sawtimber volume—Net volume of sawtimber trees measured in board feet. Softwood volume is estimated from the top of a stump 12 inches tall up to a minimum 6-inch top diameter, inside bark, and hardwood volume is estimated from the top of a stump 12 inches tall up to a minimum 8-inch top diameter, inside bark. Net sawtimber volume equals gross volume less deduction for rot, sweep, crook, and other defects that affect use for lumber.

Scribner rule—The common board-foot log rule used locally in western Oregon to determine sawtimber volume. Scribner volume is estimated in terms of 32-foot logs for softwoods and 16-foot logs for hardwoods. See "sawtimber volume" for utilization limits.

Site class—A classification of the potential productivity of forest land expressed as mean annual increment (MAI) at culmination in fully stocked natural stands. Six classes in this report are based on a range of MAI values that were calculated on every plot.

Site index—A measure of the productivity of forest land expressed as the average height of dominant and codominant trees at a specified age.

Softwoods—Coniferous trees, usually evergreen, with needles or scalelike leaves. See "Names of Trees" for a list of softwood species in this report.

Stand age—The 10-year age class that best characterizes the stand. See "even-aged stand" and "uneven-aged stand" for more details.

Stand-size class—A classification of stands based on tree size. Stand-size classes are sawtimber, poletimber, and sapling-seedling stands.

State lands—Lands owned by states or administered by state agencies.

Timber harvest—Volume of roundwood removed from forest land for products. Timber harvest statistics reported in tables 30a through 30d were collected by the Oregon Department of Forestry.

Timber volume—Includes the net volume in cubic feet of poletimber and sawtimber trees and salvable dead sawtimber trees, and the net volume in cubic feet of cull trees of commercial species. In tables 18a-18d, the volume of cull trees includes the gross volume of noncommercial species. Volume is measured from the top of a stump 12 inches tall to a minimum 4-inch top diameter, inside bark.

Timberland—Forest land capable of growing 20 cubic feet or more per acre per year (mean annual increment at culmination in fully stocked, natural stands) of industrial wood and not in a reserved status through removal of the area from timber utilization by statute, ordinance, or administrative order and not in a withdrawn status where it is pending consideration for reserved status.

Uneven-aged stands—Stands where less than 70 percent of the tree stocking falls in three adjacent 10-year age classes.

Upper stem portion—The bole of sawtimber trees above the saw-log top—7.0 inches diameter outside bark for softwoods and 9.0 inches diameter outside bark for hardwoods—to a minimum top diameter of 4.0 inches inside bark, or to the point where the central stem divides into limbs.

Names of Trees

Common name	Scientific name[1]
Softwoods:	
Alaska-cedar	*Chamaecyparis nootkatensis* (D. Don) Spach
Brewer spruce	*Picea brewerana* [*breweriana*] Wats.
Douglas-fir	*Pseudotsuga menziesii* (Mirb.) Franco
Engelmann spruce	*Picea engelmannii* Parry ex Engelm.
Giant sequoia	*Sequoiadendron giganteum* (Lindl.) Buchh.
Grand fir	*Abies grandis* (Dougl. ex D. Don) Lindl.
Incense-cedar	*Libocedrus decurrens* Torr.
Jeffrey pine	*Pinus jeffreyi* Grev. & Balf.
Knobcone pine	*Pinus attenuata* Lemm.
Lodgepole pine	*Pinus contorta* Dougl. ex Loud.
Mountain hemlock	*Tsuga mertensiana* (Bong.) Carr.
Noble fir	*Abies procera* Rehd.
Pacific silver fir	*Abies amabilis* Dougl. ex Forbes
Ponderosa pine	*Pinus ponderosa* Dougl. ex Laws.
Port-Orford-cedar	*Chamaecyparis lawsoniana* (A Murr.) Parl.
Redwood	*Sequoia sempervirens* (D. Don) Endl.
Scotch pine	*Pinus sylvestris* L.
Shasta red fir	*Abies shastensis* (Lemmon)
Sitka spruce	*Picea sitchensis* (Bong.) Carr.
Subalpine fir	*Abies lasiocarpa* (Hook.) Nutt.
Sugar pine	*Pinus lambertiana* Dougl.
Western hemlock	*Tsuga heterophylla* (Raf.) Sarg.
Western juniper	*Juniperus occidentalis* Hook.
Western redcedar	*Thuja plicata* Donn ex D. Don
Western white pine	*Pinus monticola* Dougl. ex D. Don
White fir	*Abies concolor* (Gord. & Glend.) Lindl. ex Hildebr.
Whitebark pine	*Pinus albicaulis* Engelm.
Hardwoods:	
Apple	*Malus* spp. Mill.
Bigleaf maple	*Acer macrophyllum* Pursh
Black cottonwood	*Populus trichocarpa* (Torr. & Gray)
Black locust	*Robinia pseudoacacia* L.
California black oak	*Quercus kelloggii* Newb.
California-laurel	*Umbellularia californica* (Hook. & Arn.) Nutt.
Canyon live oak	*Quercus chrysolepis* Liebm.
Cherry	*Prunus* spp.
Golden chinkapin	*Chrysolepis chrysophylla* (Dougl. ex Hook.) Hjelmqvist
Holly	*Ilex* spp.
Oregon ash	*Fraxinus latifolia* Benth.
Oregon white oak	*Quercus garryana* Dougl. ex Hook.
Quaking aspen	*Populus tremuloides* Michx.
Pacific madrone	*Arbutus menziesii* Pursh
Red alder	*Alnus rubra* Bong.
Tanoak	*Lithocarpus densiflorus* (Hook. & Arn.) Rehd.
White alder	*Alnus rhombifolia* Nutt.
Willow	*Salix* spp.

[1] Nomenclature per Little (1979).

Acknowledgments

Many people were involved in the collection of data and the design of the inventory. Thanks go to the data collection staff: Brett Anderson, Christina Anthony, Joy Archuleta, Dale Baer, Jennifer Baker, Del Barge, Adam Blackwood, Steve Bolon, Sarah Butler, Perry Colclasure, Shaun Curtis, Brian Daum, Sebastien DeLion, Peter DelZotto, Paul Dunham, Szilard Farkas, Perttu Finni, Andrei Fiodorov, Jennifer Gomoll, Walter Grabowiecki, Erica Hanson, Kalle Harkonen, Sarah Hedrich, Mike Hogan, Ellie Husk, Jari Jokinen, Dana Katz, Juha Kauppila, Kim Kuhne, J.D. Lloyd, Kitty McCovey, Tom Meade, Cecilia Meyers, Scott Nelson, Dominic Ortiz, Mikko Paivinen, Melissa Patterson, Aimee Porcaro, Bob Rhoads, Tony Rodriguez, Sam Solano, Julie Theil, Chuck Veneklase, Mark Weber, and Len Zeoli. Thanks go to Chuck Bolsinger, Gary Lettman, and Neil McKay who provided valuable reviews. Dale Weyermann provided the maps and Paul Dunham the cover photograph. A special thanks to the many landowners who allowed field crews on their lands to visit plots and measure trees.

Metric Equivalents

1 acre = 0.405 hectare

1 acre = 4046.86 square meters

1,000 acres = 404.7 hectares

1,000 cubic feet = 28.3 cubic meters

1 cubic foot per acre = 0.07 cubic meter per hectare

1 foot = 0.3048 meter

1 inch = 2.54 centimeters

1 mile = 1.609 kilometers

Literature Cited

Bassett, P.M. 1977. Timber resources of southwest Oregon. Resour. Bull. PNW-RB-72. Portland, OR: U.S. Department of Agriculture, Forest Service, Pacific Northwest Forest and Range Experiment Station. 29 p.

Cochran, W.G. 1977. Sampling techniques. 3rd ed. New York: John Wiley & Sons. 413 p.

Gedney, D.R.; Bassett, P.M.; Mei, M.A. 1986a. Timber resource statistics for nonfederal forest land in southwest Oregon. Resour. Bull. PNW-138. Portland, OR: U.S. Department of Agriculture, Forest Service, Pacific Northwest Research Station. 26 p.

Gedney, D.R.; Bassett, P.M.; Mei, M.A. 1986b. Timber resource statistics for nonfederal forest land in northwest Oregon. Resour. Bull. PNW-RB-140. Portland, OR: U.S. Department of Agriculture, Forest Service, Pacific Northwest Research Station. 26 p.

Gedney, D.R.; Bassett, P.M.; Mei, M.A. 1987. Timber resource statistics for nonfederal forest land in west-central Oregon. Resour. Bull. PNW-RB-143. Portland, OR: U.S. De-partment of Agriculture, Forest Service, Pacific Northwest Research Station. 26 p.

Hazard, J.W.; Metcalf, M.E. 1964. Forest statistics for southwest Oregon. Resour. Bull. PNW-8. Portland, OR: U.S. Department of Agriculture, Forest Service, Pacific Northwest Forest and Range Experiment Station. 32 p.

Hazard, J.W.; Metcalf, M.E. 1965. Forest statistics for west-central Oregon. Resour. Bull. PNW-10. Portland, OR: U.S. Department of Agriculture, Forest Service, Pacific Northwest Forest and Range Experiment Station. 35 p.

Jacobs, D.M. 1978. Timber resources of west-central Oregon. Resour. Bull. PNW-76. Portland, OR: U.S. Department of Agriculture, Forest Service, Pacific Northwest Forest and Range Experiment Station. 30 p.

Little, E.L., Jr. 1979. Checklist of United States trees (native and naturalized). Agric. Handb. 541. Washington, DC: U.S. Department of Agriculture, Forest Service. 375 p.

Max, T.A.; Schreuder, H.T.; Hazard, J.W. [and others]. 1996. The Pacific Northwest Region vegetation and inventory monitoring system. Res. Pap. PNW-RP-493. Portland, OR: U.S. Department of Agriculture, Forest Service, Pacific Northwest Research Station. 22 p.

McKay, N.; Bolsinger, C.L.; Lettman, G.J. [and others]. 1998. Timber resource trends on nonfederal timberland in western Oregon between 1984-86 and 1994. Salem, OR: Oregon Department of Forestry. 126 p.

Mei, M.A. 1979. Timber resources of northwest Oregon. Resour. Bull. PNW-82. Portland, OR: U.S. Department of Agriculture, Forest Service, Pacific Northwest Forest and Range Experiment Station. 29 p.

Metcalf, M.E.; Hazard, J.W. 1964. Forest statistics for northwest Oregon. Resour. Bull. PNW-7. Portland, OR: U.S. Department of Agriculture, Forest Service, Pacific Northwest Forest and Range Experiment Station. 38 p.

U.S. Department of Commerce, Bureau of the Census. 1990. 1990 census of population. Vol. 1: characteristics of the population. Part 1: United States summary. Washington, DC: [Pages unknown].

Table 1—Estimated land area by county, land class, and administrative status, western Oregon, January 1, 1997[a b]

County	Timberland	Reserved timberland	Available other forest	Reserved other forest	Total forest	Non-forest	All land[c]
			Thousand acres				
Northwest:							
Clackamas	778	87	28	—	893	303	1,196
Clatsop	460	—	28	4	492	37	529
Columbia	310	—	27	—	337	83	420
Hood River	186	—	15	—	201	133	334
Marion	308	68	18	13	407	351	758
Multnomah	104	24	—	12	140	139	279
Polk	262	—	4	—	266	208	474
Tillamook	617	8	11	—	636	69	705
Washington	244	—	8	7	259	204	463
Yamhill	212	—	23	6	241	217	458
Total	3,481	187	162	42	3,872	1,744	5,616
West central:							
Benton	318	1	3	—	322	111	433
Lane	2,165	241	45	6	2,457	464	2,921
Lincoln	547	6	16	—	569	66	635
Linn	918	66	39	—	1,023	443	1,466
Total	3,948	314	103	6	4,371	1,084	5,455
Southwest:							
Coos	842	15	21	1	879	145	1,024
Curry	763	185	9	19	976	66	1,042
Douglas	2,516	96	146	7	2,765	459	3,224
Jackson	1,158	64	264	15	1,501	282	1,783
Josephine	803	64	59	11	937	112	1,049
Total	6,082	424	499	53	7,058	1,064	8,122
Total	13,511	925	764	101	15,301	3,892	19,193

— = less than 500 acres.

[a] Totals may be off because of rounding; data subject to sampling error.

[b] Includes data for the national forests and BLM from their regional surveys, submitted to 1997 RPA.

[c] Source: U.S. Department of Commerce 1990.

Table 2a—Estimated area of nonfederal reserved timberland and other forest land by forest type, western Oregon, January 1, 1997[a]

Forest type	Reserved timberland	Other forest		Total
		Available	Reserved	
		Thousand acres		
Softwood types:				
Douglas-fir	7	186	16	209
Grand fir	—	11	7	18
Incense-cedar	—	9	—	9
Lodgepole pine	—	31	5	36
Pacific silver fir	—	8	—	8
Scotch pine	—	2	—	2
Sitka spruce	7	—	7	14
Western hemlock	—	4	—	4
Western juniper	—	4	—	4
Total	14	255	35	304
Hardwood types:				
Bigleaf maple	—	9	16	25
Black cottonwood	—	8	6	13
California black oak	—	24	—	24
Oregon ash	—	7	—	7
Oregon white oak	—	193	5	198
Pacific madrone	—	46	—	46
Red alder	—	11	3	14
Tanoak	—	7	—	7
White alder	—	5	—	5
Willow	—	13	—	13
Total	—	322	29	352
Nonstocked[b]	—	34	—	34
All types	14	611	64	690

— = less than 500 acres found.
[a] Totals may be off because of rounding; data subject to sampling error.
[b] Nonstocked areas are less than 10 percent stocked with live trees.

Table 2b—Estimated area of nonfederal reserved timberland and other forest land by forest type, northwest Oregon, January 1, 1997[a]

| Forest type | Reserved timberland | Other forest | | Total |
		Available	Reserved	
		Thousand acres		
Softwood types:				
Douglas-fir	—	53	9	62
Grand fir	—	—	7	7
Lodgepole pine	—	16	—	16
Sitka spruce	—	—	—	—
Western hemlock	—	4	—	4
Total	—	73	16	89
Hardwood types:				
Bigleaf maple	—	—	16	16
Black cottonwood	—	6	6	12
Oregon ash	—	4	—	4
Oregon white oak	—	30	—	30
Red alder	—	11	3	14
Willow	—	13	—	13
Total	—	63	24	88
Nonstocked[b]	—	10	—	10
All types	—	146	40	187

— = less than 500 acres found.

[a] Totals may be off because of rounding; data subject to sampling error.

[b] Nonstocked areas are less than 10 percent stocked with live trees.

Table 2c—Estimated area of nonfederal reserved timberland and other forest land by forest type, west-central Oregon, January 1, 1997[a]

Forest type	Reserved timberland	Other forest		Total
		Available	Reserved	
		Thousand acres		
Softwood types:				
Douglas-fir	—	55	6	61
Lodgepole pine	—	6	—	6
Pacific silver fir	—	8	—	8
Scotch pine	—	2	—	2
Western hemlock	—	5	—	5
Total	—	76	6	82
Hardwood types:				
Black cottonwood	—	2	—	2
Golden chinkapin	—	5	—	5
Oregon white oak	—	10	—	10
Pacific madrone	—	1	—	1
Total	—	18	—	18
Nonstocked[b]	—	12	—	12
All types	—	106	6	112

— = less than 500 acres found.
[a] Totals may be off because of rounding; data subject to sampling error.
[b] Nonstocked areas are less than 10 percent stocked with live trees.

Table 2d—Estimated area of nonfederal reserved timberland and other forest land by forest type, southwest Oregon, January 1, 1997[a]

Forest type	Reserved timberland	Other forest		Total
		Available	Reserved	
		Thousand acres		
Softwood types:				
Douglas-fir	7	77	—	84
Grand fir	—	11	—	11
Incense-cedar	—	9	—	9
Lodgepole pine	—	9	5	14
Port-Orford-cedar	2	—	—	2
Sitka spruce	7	—	7	14
Western juniper	—	4	—	4
Total	15	110	12	137
Hardwood types:				
Bigleaf maple	—	9	—	9
California black oak	—	24	—	24
Oregon ash	—	3	—	3
Oregon white oak	—	153	5	158
Pacific madrone	—	45	—	45
Tanoak	—	7	—	7
White alder	—	5	—	5
Total	—	246	5	251
Nonstocked[b]	—	12	—	12
All types	15	368	16	400

— = less than 500 acres found.

[a] Totals may be off because of rounding; data subject to sampling error.

[b] Nonstocked areas are less than 10 percent stocked with live trees.

Table 3—Estimated area of timberland by county and owner class, western Oregon, January 1, 1997[a][b]

County	Public						Private				
	National forest	Bureau of Land Management	Miscellaneous federal	State	County	Total public	Forest industry	Native American	Miscellaneous private	Total private	All owners
						Thousand acres					
Northwest Oregon:											
Clackamas	438	51	—	6	6	501	130	—	156	286	787
Clatsop	—	—	—	112	6	118	258	—	45	303	421
Columbia	—	11	1	—	—	12	214	—	83	297	309
Hood River	121	—	—	—	19	140	31	—	14	45	185
Marion	147	21	—	30	—	198	48	—	62	110	308
Multnomah	50	4	—	—	—	54	15	—	34	49	103
Polk	1	40	—	—	—	41	142	—	79	221	262
Tillamook	87	40	—	302	11	440	134	—	44	178	618
Washington	—	12	—	80	—	92	44	—	108	152	244
Yamhill	26	32	—	—	—	58	86	—	68	154	212
Total	870	211	1	530	42	1,654	1,102	—	692	1,795	3,449
West-central Oregon:											
Benton	18	66	—	28	—	112	159	—	46	205	317
Lane	1,095	267	5	45	—	1,412	557	—	207	764	2,176
Lincoln	166	20	—	22	—	208	266	18	56	340	548
Linn	367	83	—	7	—	457	357	—	103	460	917
Total	1,646	436	5	102	—	2,189	1,339	18	413	1,769	3,958
Southwest Oregon:											
Coos	69	154	—	63	9	295	403	—	144	547	842
Curry	418	53	—	—	—	471	217	—	75	292	763
Douglas	902	595	—	42	7	1,546	748	—	322	1,070	2,616
Jackson	392	324	5	11	11	743	308	—	111	419	1,162
Josephine	317	283	—	—	35	635	61	—	107	168	803
Total	2,098	1,409	5	116	62	3,690	1,736	—	759	2,496	6,186
Total	4,614	2,056	11	748	104	7,533	4,177	18	1,864	6,060	13,593

— = less than 500 acres.

[a] Totals may be off because of rounding; data subject to sampling error.

[b] Data for the national forests and BLM is from their regional surveys, submitted to 1997 RPA.

Table 4a—Estimated area of nonfederal timberland, by forest type and owner class, western Oregon, January 1, 1997[a]

Forest type	Other public	Forest industry	Other private	All owners
	Thousand acres			
Softwood types:				
Douglas-fir	573	2,792	947	4,313
Grand fir	—	39	23	63
Incense-cedar	—	41	39	79
Jeffrey pine	—	—	2	2
Noble fir	6	18	—	24
Pacific silver fir	—	8	—	8
Ponderosa pine	—	3	17	20
Port-Orford-cedar	—	8	11	19
Redwood	—	2	—	2
Sitka spruce	13	56	40	109
Western hemlock	46	360	31	437
Western redcedar	3	24	28	55
White fir	—	55	2	58
Total softwood types	642	3,407	1,141	5,190
Hardwood types:				
Apple	—	2	2	4
Bigleaf maple	12	50	96	157
Black cottonwood	—	6	7	13
California black oak	—	6	33	39
California-laurel	—	19	—	19
Canyon live oak	—	41	—	41
Cherry	. 1	—	3	5
Oregon ash	—	6	19	25
Oregon white oak	5	54	93	152
Pacific madrone	35	77	116	227
Red alder	150	309	264	723
Tanoak	—	105	19	124
Willow	—	2	12	13
Total hardwood types	203	678	663	1,544
Nonstocked[b]	6	37	58	101
Not classified[c]	—	57	18	75
All types	850	4,179	1,880	6,909

— = less than 500 acres found.

[a] Totals may be off because of rounding; data subject to sampling error.

[b] Nonstocked areas are less than 10 percent stocked with live trees.

[c] Unclassified areas include access-denied areas that were harvested since the last inventory.

Table 4b—Estimated area of nonfederal timberland, by forest type and owner class, northwest Oregon, January 1, 1997[a]

Forest type	Other public	Forest industry	Other private	All owners
	Thousand acres			
Softwood types:				
Douglas-fir	379	665	343	1,387
Grand fir	—	—	5	5
Incense-cedar	—	—	2	2
Noble fir	6	10	—	16
Pacific silver fir	—	8	—	8
Sitka spruce	13	32	10	55
Western hemlock	46	227	15	288
Western redcedar	3	14	18	36
Total softwood types	448	956	394	1,798
Hardwood types:				
Apple	—	—	2	2
Bigleaf maple	12	10	68	90
Black cottonwood	—	6	7	13
Cherry	1	—	3	5
Oregon ash	—	—	6	6
Oregon white oak	—	—	49	49
Red alder	107	70	139	317
Total hardwood types	121	87	274	481
Nonstocked[b]	5	15	22	42
Unclassified[c]	—	45	2	47
Total all types	574	1,104	691	2,368

— = less than 500 acres found.

[a] Totals may be off because of rounding; data subject to sampling error.

[b] Nonstocked areas are less than 10 percent stocked with live trees.

[c] Unclassified areas include access-denied areas that were harvested since the last inventory.

Table 4c—Estimated area of nonfederal timberland, by forest type and owner class, west-central Oregon, January 1, 1997[a]

Forest type	Other public	Forest industry	Other private	All owners
	Thousand acres			
Softwood types:				
Douglas-fir	68	1,007	227	1,302
Grand fir	—	19	7	26
Incense-cedar	—	2	—	2
Noble fir	—	8	—	8
Ponderosa pine	—	—	1	1
Sitka spruce	—	18	20	38
Western hemlock	—	107	14	121
Western redcedar	—	1	3	4
Total softwood types	68	1,162	272	1,502
Hardwood types:				
Bigleaf maple	—	21	23	44
California black oak	—	—	5	5
Oregon ash	—	1	13	14
Oregon white oak	5	34	14	53
Pacific madrone	8	—	5	13
Red alder	16	96	53	165
Total hardwood types	29	152	113	294
Nonstocked[b]	—	14	29	43
Not classified[c]	—	12	16	28
All types	97	1,339	430	1,867

— = less than 500 acres found.

[a] Totals may be off because of rounding; data subject to sampling error.

[b] Nonstocked areas are less than 10 percent stocked with live trees.

[c] Unclassified areas include access-denied areas that were harvested since the last inventory.

Table 4d—Estimated area of nonfederal timberland, by forest type and owner class, southwest Oregon, January 1, 1997[a]

Forest type	Other public	Forest industry	Other private	All owners
	Thousand acres			
Softwood types:				
Douglas-fir	125	1,121	377	1,623
Grand fir	—	20	11	31
Incense-cedar	—	38	37	75
Jeffrey pine	—	—	2	2
Ponderosa pine	—	3	16	19
Port-Orford-cedar	—	8	11	19
Redwood	—	2	—	2
Sitka spruce	—	6	10	17
Western hemlock	—	26	2	28
Western redcedar	—	9	6	15
White fir	—	55	2	58
Total softwood types	125	1,289	476	1,890
Hardwood types:				
Apple	—	2	—	2
Bigleaf maple	—	19	5	23
California black oak	—	6	28	34
California-laurel	—	19	0	19
Canyon live oak	—	41	—	41
Oregon ash	—	5	—	5
Oregon white oak	—	20	30	50
Pacific madrone	27	77	110	214
Red alder	26	143	72	241
Tanoak	—	105	19	124
Willow	—	2	12	13
Total hardwood types	53	439	276	768
Nonstocked[b]	—	8	7	15
All types	179	1,736	759	2,809

— = less than 500 acres found.

[a] Totals may be off because of rounding; data subject to sampling error.

[b] Nonstocked areas are less than 10 percent stocked with live trees.

Table 5a—Estimated area of nonfederal timberland, by owner class, stand-size class, and forest type group, western Oregon, January 1, 1997[a]

Stand-size class	Other public	Forest industry	Other private	All owners
	Thousand acres			
Large sawtimber:				
Softwood types	75	127	118	320
Hardwood type	12	3	16	31
All types	87	130	134	351
Small sawtimber:				
Softwood types	436	1,691	619	2,746
Hardwood types	110	241	276	627
All types	546	1,932	895	3,373
Poletimber:				
Softwood types	43	435	108	586
Hardwood types	45	247	177	469
All types	88	682	285	1,055
Seedlings and saplings:				
Softwood types	88	1,155	296	1,539
Hardwood types	35	187	193	415
All types	123	1,342	489	1,954
All stand-size classes:				
Softwood types	642	3,408	1,141	5,191
Hardwood types	202	678	662	1,542
Nonstocked[b]	6	37	58	101
All types[c]	850	4,123	1,861	6,834

— = less than 500 acres found.

[a] Totals may be off because of rounding; data subject to sampling error.

[b] Stand-size class was not determined for nonstocked stands.

[c] Total does not include 75,000 acres of unclassified access-denied lands.

Table 5b–Estimated area of nonfederal timberland, by owner class, stand-size class, and forest type group, northwest Oregon, January 1, 1997[a]

Stand-size class	Other public	Forest industry	Other private	All owners
	Thousand acres			
Large sawtimber:				
Softwood types	31	26	71	128
Hardwood types	8	—	9	17
All types	39	26	80	145
Small sawtimber:				
Softwood types	337	562	195	1,094
Hardwood types	90	58	130	278
All types	427	620	325	1,372
Poletimber:				
Softwood types	26	94	16	136
Hardwood types	22	12	63	97
All types	48	106	79	233
Seedlings and saplings:				
Softwood types	54	275	111	440
Hardwood types	—	16	72	88
All types	54	291	183	528
All stand-size classes:				
Softwood types	448	957	393	1,798
Hardwood types	120	86	274	480
Nonstocked[b]	5	15	22	42
All types[c]	573	1,058	689	2,320

— = less than 500 acres found.

[a] Totals may be off because of rounding; data subject to sampling error.

[b] Stand-size class was not determined for nonstocked stands.

[c] Total does not include 47,000 acres of unclassified access-denied lands.

Table 5c–Estimated area of nonfederal timberland, by owner class, stand-size class, and forest type group, west-central Oregon, January 1, 1997[a]

Stand-size class	Other public	Forest industry	Other private	All owners
	Thousand acres			
Large sawtimber:				
Softwood types	6	57	32	95
Hardwood types	—	—	7	7
All types	6	57	39	102
Small sawtimber:				
Softwood types	35	557	143	735
Hardwood types	—	58	57	115
All types	35	615	200	850
Poletimber:				
Softwood types	12	143	25	180
Hardwood types	14	62	11	87
All types	26	205	36	267
Seedlings and saplings:				
Softwood types	16	406	71	493
Hardwood types	15	32	37	84
All types	31	438	108	577
All stand-size classes:				
Softwood types	69	1,163	271	1,503
Hardwood types	29	152	112	293
Nonstocked[b]	—	14	29	43
All types[c]	98	1,329	412	1,839

— = less than 500 acres found.
[a] Totals may be off because of rounding; data subject to sampling error.
[b] Stand-size class was not determined for nonstocked stands.
[c] Total does not include 28,000 acres of unclassified access-denied lands.

Table 5d–Estimated area of nonfederal timberland, by owner class, stand-size class, and forest type group, southwest Oregon, January 1, 1997[a]

Stand-size class	Other public	Forest industry	Other private	All owners
	Thousand acres			
Large sawtimber:				
Softwood types	38	45	15	98
Hardwood types	4	3	—	7
All types	42	48	15	105
Small sawtimber:				
Softwood types	64	573	281	918
Hardwood types	19	124	89	232
All types	83	697	370	1,150
Poletimber:				
Softwood types	4	198	66	268
Hardwood types	9	174	103	286
All types	13	372	169	554
Seedlings and saplings:				
Softwood types	18	474	113	606
Hardwood types	20	138	84	242
All types	38	612	197	847
All stand-size classes:				
Softwood types	124	1,290	475	1,889
Hardwood types	52	439	276	767
Nonstocked[b]	—	65	7	72
All types	176	1,794	758	2,728

— = less than 500 acres found.

[a] Totals may be off because of rounding; data subject to sampling error.

[b] Stand-size class was not determined for nonstocked stands.

Table 6a—Estimated area of timberland, by cubic-foot site class and owner class, western Oregon, January 1, 1997[a b]

| Owner | Site class[c] | | | | | | All classes |
	≥225	165-224	120-164	85-119	50-84	20-49	
	Thousand acres						
National forest	51	525	1,355	1,152	1,415	115	4,612
BLM	9	240	960	444	384	14	2,052
Other public	44	400	278	76	53	0	851
Forest industry	310	1,628	1,370	568	254	47	4,177
Other private	89	433	708	336	224	91	1,881
All owners	503	3,226	4,671	2,576	2,330	268	13,573

[a] Totals may be off because of rounding; data subject to sampling error.
[b] National forest and BLM data are estimated by using the 1977 percentage area by site class applied to the present acreage.
[c] Site class is the mean annual increment cubic-foot growth per acre at culmination in fully stocked natural stands.

Table 6b—Estimated area of timberland, by cubic-foot site class and owner class, northwest Oregon, January 1, 1997[a b]

| Owner | Site class[c] | | | | | | All classes |
	≥225	165-224	120-164	85-119	50-84	20-49	
	Thousand acres						
National forest	18	84	251	194	314	5	867
BLM	4	23	132	39	12	0	210
Other public	44	307	166	45	13	0	575
Forest industry	202	442	360	95	4	0	1,103
Other private	51	159	330	126	22	4	692
All owners	319	1,015	1,240	499	365	9	3,447

[a] Totals may be off because of rounding; data subject to sampling error.
[b] National forest and BLM data are estimated by using the 1977 percentage area by site class applied to the present acreage.
[c] Site class is the mean annual increment cubic-foot growth per acre at culmination in fully stocked natural stands.

Table 6c—Estimated area of timberland, by cubic-foot site class and owner class, west-central Oregon, January 1, 1997[a][b]

Owner	Site class[c]						All classes
	≥225	165-224	120-164	85-119	50-84	20-49	
	Thousand acres						
National forest	22	325	587	366	322	22	1,644
BLM	2	67	291	50	26	0	436
Other public	0	39	47	13	0	0	99
Forest industry	63	655	459	135	20	8	1,340
Other private	18	158	175	50	29	0	430
All owners	105	1,244	1,559	615	397	30	3,949

— less than 500 acres.
[a] Totals may be off because of rounding; data subject to sampling error.
[b] National forest and BLM data are estimated by using the 1977 percentage area by site class applied to the present acreage.
[c] Site class is the mean annual increment cubic-foot growth per acre at culmination in fully stocked natural stands.

Table 6d—Estimated area of timberland, by cubic-foot site class and owner class, southwest Oregon, January 1, 1997[a][b]

Owner	Site class[c]						All classes
	≥225	165-224	120-164	85-119	50-84	20-49	
	Thousand acres						
National forest	11	111	513	594	779	90	2,099
BLM	3	149	525	360	355	15	1,407
Other public	0	55	66	18	39	0	178
Forest industry	46	531	552	338	230	39	1,736
Other private	20	117	203	160	172	87	759
All owners	80	963	1,860	1,469	1,574	231	6,178

[a] Totals may be off because of rounding; data subject to sampling error.
[b] National forest and BLM data are estimated by using the 1977 percentage area by site class applied to the present acreage.
[c] Site class is the mean annual increment cubic-foot growth per acre at culmination in fully stocked natural stands.

Table 7a—Estimated area of nonfederal timberland, by forest type and stand-size class, western Oregon, January 1, 1997[a]

Forest type	Large sawtimber	Small sawtimber	Pole-timber	Seedling-sapling	All classes
	Thousand acres				
Softwood types:					
Douglas-fir	237	2,289	478	1,308	4,313
Grand fir	9	27	—	26	63
Incense-cedar	7	22	22	29	79
Jeffrey pine	2	—	—	—	2
Noble fir	—	6	6	12	24
Pacific silver fir	—	—	8	—	8
Ponderosa pine	13	—	8	—	20
Port-Orford-cedar	—	16	3	—	19
Redwood	—	2	—	—	2
Sitka spruce	36	54	4	16	109
Western hemlock	1	277	59	100	437
Western redcedar	29	21	—	5	55
White fir	1	34	—	22	58
Total	321	2,746	585	1,538	5,190
Hardwood types:					
Apple		—	2	2	4
Bigleaf maple	11	58	47	42	157
Black cottonwood	6	—	7	—	13
California black oak	14	25	—	—	39
California-laurel	15	5	—	—	19
Canyon live oak	—	13	28	—	41
Cherry	—	—	1	3	5
Oregon ash	4	6	—	15	25
Oregon white oak	2	66	40	44	152
Pacific madrone	46	96	85	—	227
Red alder	12	377	202	132	723
Tanoak	3	32	37	52	124
Willow	—	5	2	6	13
Total	31	626	470	415	1,544
Nonstocked[b]	—	—	—	—	101
Unclassified[c]	—	—	—	—	75
All types	352	3,724	1,055	1,954	6,909

— = less than 500 acres found.

[a] Totals may be off because of rounding; data subject to sampling error.

[b] Nonstocked areas are less than 10 percent stocked with live trees.

[c] Unclassified lands are areas where access was denied.

Table 7b—Estimated area of nonfederal timberland, by forest type and stand-size class, northwest Oregon, January 1, 1997[a]

Forest type	Large sawtimber	Small sawtimber	Pole-timber	Seedling-sapling	All classes
	Thousand acres				
Softwood types:					
Douglas-fir	96	854	87	350	1,387
Grand fir	—	5	—	—	5
Incense-cedar	—	—	—	2	2
Noble fir	—	6	6	4	16
Pacific silver fir	—	—	—	8	8
Sitka spruce	2	35	4	14	55
Western hemlock	1	191	40	56	288
Western redcedar	28	2	—	5	36
Total	128	1,093	137	440	1,798
Hardwood types:					
Apple	—	—	2	—	2
Bigleaf maple	7	46	6	30	90
Black cottonwood	—	6	—	7	13
Cherry	—	—	1	3	5
Oregon ash	—	6	—	—	6
Oregon white oak	2	16	23	9	49
Red alder	8	203	65	40	317
Total	17	279	97	88	481
Nonstocked[b]	—	—	—	—	42
Unclassified[c]	—	—	—	—	47
All types	145	1,372	234	528	2,369

— = less than 500 acres found.

[a] Totals may be off because of rounding; data subject to sampling error.

[b] Nonstocked areas are less than 10 percent stocked with live trees.

[c] Unclassified lands are areas where access was denied.

Table 7c—Estimated area of nonfederal timberland, by forest type and stand-size class, west-central Oregon, January 1, 1997[a]

Forest type	Large sawtimber	Small sawtimber	Pole-timber	Seedling-sapling	All classes
	Thousand acres				
Softwood types:					
Douglas-fir	67	631	170	435	1,302
Grand fir	—	7	—	19	26
Incense-cedar	2	—	—	—	2
Noble fir	—	—	—	8	8
Ponderosa pine	—	1	—	—	1
Sitka spruce	24	13	—	—	38
Western hemlock	—	80	10	31	121
Western redcedar	1	3	—	—	4
Total	95	735	180	493	1,502
Hardwood types:					
Bigleaf maple	4	4	27	9	44
California black oak	—	5	—	—	5
Oregon ash	4	—	—	10	14
Oregon white oak	—	26	13	14	53
Pacific madrone	—	—	—	13	13
Red alder	—	79	47	39	165
Total	7	115	87	85	294
Nonstocked[b]	—	—	—	—	43
Unclassified[c]	—	—	—	—	28
All types	102	850	267	577	1,867

— = less than 500 acres found.

[a] Totals may be off because of rounding; data subject to sampling error.

[b] Nonstocked areas are less than 10 percent stocked with live trees.

[c] Unclassified lands are areas where access was denied.

Table 7d—Estimated area of nonfederal timberland, by forest type and stand-size class, southwest Oregon, January 1, 1997[a]

Forest type	Large sawtimber	Small sawtimber	Pole-timber	Seedling-sapling	All classes
	Thousand acres				
Softwood types:					
Douglas-fir	75	804	222	523	1,623
Grand fir	9	15	—	7	31
Incense-cedar	5	22	22	27	75
Jeffrey pine	—	2	—	—	2
Ponderosa pine	—	12	—	8	19
Port-Orford-cedar	—	—	16	3	19
Redwood	—	2	—	—	2
Sitka spruce	9	6	—	2	17
Western hemlock	—	6	9	13	28
Western redcedar	—	15	—	—	15
White fir	1	34	—	22	58
Total	98	918	268	606	1,890
Hardwood types:					
Apple	—	—	—	2	2
Bigleaf maple	—	7	14	2	23
California black oak	—	9	25	—	34
California-laurel	—	15	5	—	19
Canyon live oak	—	—	13	28	41
Oregon ash	—	—	—	5	5
Oregon white oak	—	24	5	21	50
Pacific madrone	—	46	96	72	214
Red alder	4	95	90	53	241
Tanoak	3	32	37	52	124
Willow	—	5	2	6	13
Total	7	233	286	242	768
Nonstocked[b]	—	—	—	—	15
All types	105	1,150	554	848	2,673

— = less than 500 acres found.

[a] Totals may be off because of rounding; data subject to sampling error.

[b] Nonstocked areas are less than 10 percent stocked with live trees.

Table 8a—Estimated number of growing-stock trees on nonfederal timberland, by species and diameter class, western Oregon, January 1, 1997[a][b]

Thousand trees

Species	1.0-2.9	3.0-4.9	5.0-6.9	7.0-8.9	9.0-10.9	11.0-12.9	13.0-14.9	15.0-16.9	17.0-18.9	19.0-20.9	21.0-28.9	29.0+	All classes
Softwood:													
Douglas-fir	238,486	191,234	144,256	111,801	91,969	66,904	48,444	34,288	22,771	15,867	23,473	5,520	995,013
Grand fir	16,055	9,401	11,435	4,931	3,096	1,553	1,350	1,545	775	583	960	84	51,767
Incense-cedar	25,990	13,201	8,385	2,983	3,348	515	1,272	624	558	365	416	156	57,813
Jeffrey pine	—	—	—	94	—	—	—	—	—	15	11	—	119
Knobcone pine	—	—	—	—	—	—	43	—	—	—	—	—	43
Lodgepole pine	289	289	—	97	68	—	34	56	42	67	—	25	1,132
Noble fir	5,404	1,653	739	695	830	257	166	310	285	193	218	—	10,566
Pacific silver fir	1,475	931	348	150	175	174	33	—	—	—	17	—	3,128
Ponderosa pine	4,651	4,171	1,903	495	854	390	777	383	244	99	269	122	14,454
Port-Orford-cedar	8,660	5,115	1,817	2,126	642	554	111	202	164	94	94	14	19,596
Redwood	—	325	—	148	166	113	96	70	18	—	72	5	1,108
Sitka spruce	6,282	5,185	2,654	2,834	2,334	2,193	1,784	1,501	1,138	698	1,157	622	28,381
Sugar pine	452	452	115	115	363	61	110	116	67	91	63	20	1,910
Western hemlock	68,562	45,438	33,380	26,112	17,839	14,966	11,995	7,526	3,298	2,075	2,809	372	234,370
Western redcedar	20,279	8,102	2,983	2,056	1,969	1,263	1,168	800	471	639	1,174	707	41,608
Western white pine	—	—	—	—	—	—	—	—	25	—	—	—	25
White fir	3,810	2,521	891	1,768	1,608	1,076	582	470	264	106	152	12	13,262
Total softwoods	400,394	288,016	208,791	156,404	125,261	90,019	67,964	47,890	30,119	20,892	30,885	7,658	1,474,294
Hardwood:													
Bigleaf maple	45,551	20,489	10,550	8,400	5,703	3,798	2,249	1,776	1,313	915	1,385	306	102,435
Black cottonwood	544	845	—	113	78	60	42	—	25	43	69	81	1,900
Black locust	1,075	—	286	—	61	—	38	—	20	—	—	—	1,481
California black oak	9,746	6,884	5,241	1,910	1,474	839	537	280	297	368	244	75	27,893
California-laurel	8,652	4,740	1,653	1,182	1,522	329	224	126	54	66	78	30	18,658
Canyon live oak	16,871	3,661	1,868	454	1,107	—	179	—	—	—	—	—	24,140
Cherry	12,467	4,438	2,833	913	174	222	114	80	86	—	—	—	21,241
Golden chinkapin	25,669	10,236	5,553	3,739	1,955	758	485	—	—	—	—	—	48,482
Holly	293	—	202	110	—	—	—	—	—	—	—	—	605
Oregon ash	4,434	2,270	1,811	951	269	164	193	71	46	25	21	17	10,273
Oregon white oak	13,209	7,909	4,478	3,864	2,692	2,203	1,445	1,106	594	381	614	72	38,568
Pacific madrone	51,483	21,082	14,228	7,357	5,868	2,392	1,690	1,142	626	211	467	108	106,654
Red alder	90,519	50,218	37,275	28,050	22,675	14,787	9,831	5,467	2,834	1,580	1,625	147	265,006
Tanoak	72,005	21,990	12,111	5,970	1,951	710	628	313	425	119	253	36	116,510
White alder	—	—	134	—	—	—	—	—	—	—	—	—	134
Total hardwoods	352,517	154,761	98,222	63,013	45,529	26,262	17,656	10,361	6,320	3,708	4,756	873	783,979
All species	752,912	442,777	307,013	219,417	170,789	116,281	85,620	58,251	36,439	24,600	35,642	8,531	2,258,272

— = fewer than 500 trees found.

[a] Totals may be off because of rounding; data subject to sampling error.

[b] Growing-stock trees are all live trees except cull trees (noncommercial species are classified as sound cull trees)

Table 8b—Estimated number of growing-stock trees on nonfederal timberland, by species and diameter class, northwest Oregon, January 1, 1997[ab]

Species	Diameter class (inches at breast height)												All classes
	1.0-2.9	3.0-4.9	5.0-6.9	7.0-8.9	9.0-10.9	11.0-12.9	13.0-14.9	15.0-16.9	17.0-18.9	19.0-20.9	21.0-28.9	29.0+	
	Thousand trees												
Softwood:													
Douglas-fir	45,210	42,705	33,003	27,106	28,964	22,072	17,886	13,347	9,736	6,968	10,577	2,026	259,599
Grand fir	1,320	380	1,503	494	419	211	279	135	108	111	81	10	5,052
Noble fir	1,973	890	522	695	830	111	166	229	200	67	151	8	5,844
Pacific silver fir	738	—	348	150	175	—	33	—	—	—	17	11	1,461
Ponderosa pine	—	—	—	137	95	—	43	—	—	—	14	11	299
Sitka spruce	4,528	2,481	950	1,268	1,587	1,400	1,119	824	899	420	442	189	16,107
Western hemlock	39,642	16,645	18,433	16,018	11,012	10,095	7,551	4,901	1,865	1,064	1,671	192	129,088
Western redcedar	10,259	4,099	1,074	1,147	786	873	570	516	288	456	887	533	21,487
Total softwoods	103,671	67,200	55,834	47,015	43,866	34,763	27,647	19,951	13,095	9,084	13,840	2,969	438,936
Hardwood:													
Bigleaf maple	13,394	6,405	4,239	4,265	3,299	2,002	1,157	939	571	502	696	161	37,629
Black cottonwood	544	—	—	113	78	—	42	—	—	43	69	57	945
Black locust	1,075	—	286	—	61	—	38	—	20	—	—	—	1,481
Cherry	8,668	3,318	2,545	446	97	153	114	47	—	—	—	—	15,388
Golden chinkapin	738	—	—	—	—	—	—	—	—	—	—	—	738
Holly	293	—	202	110	—	—	—	—	—	—	—	—	605
Oregon ash	1,184	1,706	—	511	203	108	93	71	23	—	—	7	3,905
Oregon white oak	1,556	624	2,257	2,048	850	828	491	418	394	232	275	25	9,996
Pacific madrone	—	331	—	—	90	68	—	—	—	—	—	—	489
Red alder	39,704	21,523	21,198	13,928	11,059	7,241	6,091	2,772	1,566	1,002	813	59	126,957
White alder	—	—	134	—	—	—	—	—	—	—	—	—	134
Total hardwoods	67,157	33,907	30,862	21,421	15,736	10,399	8,025	4,246	2,574	1,779	1,852	308	198,267
All species	170,828	101,108	86,696	68,437	59,602	45,162	35,672	24,197	15,669	10,863	15,691	3,278	637,203

— = fewer than 500 trees found.

[a] Totals may be off because of rounding; data subject to sampling error.

[b] Growing-stock trees are all live trees except cull trees (noncommercial species are classified as sound cull trees).

Table 8c—Estimated number of growing-stock trees on nonfederal timberland, by species and diameter class, west-central Oregon, January 1, 1997[a][b]

Thousand trees

Species	Diameter class (inches at breast height)												All classes
	1.0-2.9	3.0-4.9	5.0-6.9	7.0-8.9	9.0-10.9	11.0-12.9	13.0-14.9	15.0-16.9	17.0-18.9	19.0-20.9	21.0-28.9	29.0+	
Softwood:													
Douglas-fir	52,224	45,557	35,796	35,424	27,626	19,342	12,494	8,688	6,003	4,657	6,822	1,621	256,256
Grand fir	2,573	1,959	2,111	1,283	699	316	405	209	85	128	195	9	9,971
Incense-cedar	1,544	309	552	100	160	74	84	—	86	48	41	39	3,037
Lodgepole pine	289	289	—	97	68	257	—	31	42	—	—	—	1,072
Noble fir	3,431	762	217	—	—	63	—	81	85	—	67	16	4,722
Pacific silver fir	736	931	—	—	—	—	—	—	—	—	—	—	1,667
Ponderosa pine	—	—	—	—	60	—	236	70	77	—	28	22	492
Sitka spruce	1,754	1,247	294	300	293	498	401	598	95	278	471	298	6,528
Western hemlock	22,632	20,849	10,423	7,868	5,890	3,733	3,254	2,137	1,173	694	904	113	79,670
Western redcedar	6,898	2,300	878	675	583	289	146	207	53	88	160	38	12,313
Western white pine	—	—	—	—	—	—	—	—	25	—	—	—	25
Total softwoods	92,081	74,202	50,270	45,748	35,380	24,572	17,020	12,021	7,722	5,893	8,689	2,157	375,755
Hardwood:													
Bigleaf maple	8,041	7,085	3,893	2,365	1,194	1,106	693	599	369	279	378	57	26,058
Black cottonwood	—	845	—	—	—	60	—	—	25	—	—	8	938
California black oak	—	—	700	129	472	70	42	90	75	37	42	—	1,657
Cherry	1,729	1,120	287	262	—	70	—	34	—	—	—	—	3,502
Golden chinkapin	4,204	677	119	984	1,384	553	216	—	23	25	—	11	8,193
Oregon ash	3,250	564	907	269	67	56	36	—	57	—	10	—	5,216
Oregon white oak	4,569	2,783	834	519	983	386	208	182	103	62	279	23	10,930
Pacific madrone	—	—	1,066	272	—	—	—	69	—	—	15	—	1,422
Red alder	33,559	12,004	6,048	6,359	5,549	3,572	1,452	1,353	615	217	417	88	71,232
Total hardwoods	55,349	25,078	13,854	11,159	9,650	5,873	2,647	2,326	1,266	619	1,141	186	129,149
All species	147,431	99,279	64,124	56,906	45,029	30,445	19,667	14,347	8,988	6,512	9,830	2,343	504,903

—— = fewer than 500 trees found.

[a] Totals may be off because of rounding; data subject to sampling error.

[b] Growing-stock trees are all live trees except cull trees (noncommercial species are classified as sound cull trees).

Table 8d—Estimated number of growing-stock trees on nonfederal timberland, by species and diameter class, southwest Oregon, January 1, 1997[a,b]

Species	Diameter class (inches at breast height) — *Thousand trees*												All classes
	1.0-2.9	3.0-4.9	5.0-6.9	7.0-8.9	9.0-10.9	11.0-12.9	13.0-14.9	15.0-16.9	17.0-18.9	19.0-20.9	21.0-28.9	29.0+	
Softwood:													
Douglas-fir	141,052	102,971	75,458	49,270	35,378	25,490	18,064	12,253	7,033	4,242	6,074	1,873	479,158
Grand fir	12,161	7,062	7,821	3,154	1,979	1,026	666	1,200	582	345	683	64	36,744
Incense-cedar	24,446	12,892	7,832	2,882	3,188	441	1,188	624	472	317	375	118	54,776
Jeffrey pine	—	—	—	94	—	—	—	—	—	15	11	—	119
Knobcone pine	—	—	—	—	—	—	43	—	—	—	—	—	43
Lodgepole pine	—	—	—	—	—	—	34	25	—	—	—	—	59
Ponderosa pine	4,651	4,171	1,903	358	699	390	498	313	168	193	228	90	13,662
Port-Orford-cedar	8,660	5,115	1,817	2,126	642	554	111	202	164	99	94	14	19,596
Redwood	—	325	—	148	166	113	96	70	18	94	72	5	1,108
Sitka spruce	452	1,457	1,410	1,266	454	294	264	79	143	91	245	134	5,746
Sugar pine	—	452	—	115	363	61	110	116	67	—	63	20	1,910
Western hemlock	6,288	7,944	4,524	2,226	938	1,138	1,190	488	260	317	234	66	25,612
Western redcedar	3,121	1,703	1,031	234	600	101	451	78	131	95	127	137	7,808
White fir	3,810	2,521	891	1,768	1,608	1,076	582	470	264	106	152	12	13,262
Total softwoods	204,642	146,614	102,687	63,641	46,015	30,684	23,296	15,918	9,303	5,914	8,357	2,532	659,603
Hardwood:													
Bigleaf maple	24,116	7,000	2,418	1,770	1,210	690	399	237	373	135	311	87	38,748
Black cottonwood	—	—	—	—	—	—	—	—	—	—	—	16	16
California black oak	9,746	6,884	4,541	1,781	1,002	769	495	190	222	332	201	75	26,236
California-laurel	8,652	4,740	1,653	1,182	1,522	329	224	126	54	66	78	30	18,658
Canyon live oak	16,871	3,661	1,868	454	1,107	—	179	—	—	—	—	—	24,140
Cherry	2,070	—	—	204	77	—	—	—	—	—	—	—	2,352
Golden chinkapin	20,727	9,559	5,434	2,756	571	205	269	—	30	—	11	—	39,550
Oregon ash	—	—	905	171	—	—	64	—	—	—	—	—	1,152
Oregon white oak	7,084	4,501	1,387	1,298	859	989	746	507	98	88	61	24	17,642
Pacific madrone	51,483	20,751	13,161	7,085	5,778	2,324	1,690	1,073	626	211	452	108	104,742
Red alder	17,256	16,691	10,029	7,763	6,066	3,974	2,288	1,342	653	360	396	—	66,817
Tanoak	72,005	21,990	12,111	5,970	1,951	710	628	313	425	119	253	36	116,510
Total hardwoods	230,011	95,777	53,506	30,433	20,143	9,990	6,984	3,789	2,480	1,310	1,763	378	456,563
All species	434,653	242,390	156,193	94,074	66,158	40,674	30,280	19,707	11,782	7,225	10,120	2,910	1,116,166

— = fewer than 500 trees found.

[a] Totals may be off because of rounding; data subject to sampling error.

[b] Growing-stock trees are all live trees except cull trees (noncommercial species are classified as sound cull trees).

Table 9a—Estimated net volume of growing-stock on nonfederal timberland, by species and diameter class, western Oregon, January 1, 1997[a][b]

Species	Diameter class (inches at breast height)										All classes
	5.0-6.9	7.0-8.9	9.0-10.9	11.0-12.9	13.0-14.9	15.0-16.9	17.0-18.9	19.0-20.9	21.0-28.9	29.0+	
	Million cubic feet										
Softwood:											
Douglas-fir	360	762	1,215	1,492	1,580	1,569	1,425	1,286	2,929	1,617	14,235
Grand fir	23	37	45	36	57	69	45	45	121	25	505
Incense-cedar	18	13	23	7	21	15	15	15	30	25	182
Jeffrey pine	1	—	—	—	—	—	—	1	—	2	—
Knobcone pine	—	1	—	1	—	—	—	—	—	1	—
Lodgepole pine	1	1	6	2	3	2	—	—	—	15	—
Noble fir	2	5	9	3	7	15	15	6	22	4	87
Pacific silver fir	—	—	—	—	—	—	—	—	—	—	—
Ponderosa pine	6	3	8	9	18	14	11	13	26	31	138
Port-Orford-cedar	4	9	4	7	2	5	6	4	8	—	52
Redwood	—	—	1	1	4	4	2	9	10	4	34
Sitka spruce	8	16	29	41	52	65	65	51	113	222	662
Sugar pine	1	3	1	4	3	2	4	5	5	28	—
Western hemlock	99	218	286	379	443	370	219	174	346	109	2,641
Western redcedar	6	13	26	22	32	27	24	43	114	184	490
Western white pine	—	—	—	—	—	1	—	—	1	—	—
White fir	2	10	14	16	16	17	12	8	12	3	110
Total softwoods	529	1,088	1,663	2,020	2,237	2,175	1,844	1,659	3,737	2,231	19,183
Hardwood:											
Bigleaf maple	35	54	73	88	71	83	75	69	172	116	836
Black cottonwood	—	1	1	1	2	—	1	5	11	24	45
Black locust	—	—	—	—	—	—	—	—	—	—	—
California black oak	15	13	18	16	17	11	17	25	22	19	171
California-laurel	5	8	18	6	6	4	3	4	9	6	70
Canyon live oak	5	3	6	—	5	—	—	—	—	—	19
Cherry	4	5	2	4	2	3	—	—	—	—	20
Golden chinkapin	19	29	23	13	14	—	6	—	—	—	103
Holly	—	—	—	—	—	—	—	—	—	—	—
Oregon ash	8	5	4	4	6	4	4	2	3	3	42
Oregon white oak	14	23	36	46	48	53	37	23	70	21	373
Pacific madrone	46	52	77	47	39	43	28	11	39	14	395
Red alder	117	209	341	359	348	264	163	132	162	22	2,117
Tanoak	23	24	14	8	12	8	15	6	21	7	139
White alder	1	—	—	—	—	—	—	—	—	—	1
Total hardwoods	290	426	612	592	570	474	349	277	510	232	4,332
All species	819	1,513	2,275	2,612	2,807	2,649	2,193	1,936	4,247	2,463	23,515

— = less than 500,000 cubic feet found.
[a] Totals may be off because of rounding; data subject to sampling error.
[b] Includes growing-stock trees 5.0 inches in d.b.h. and larger.

Table 9b—Estimated net volume of growing-stock on nonfederal timberland, by species and diameter class, northwest Oregon, January 1, 1997[a,b]

Species	Diameter class (inches at breast height)										All classes
	5.0-6.9	7.0-8.9	9.0-10.9	11.0-12.9	13.0-14.9	15.0-16.9	17.0-18.9	19.0-20.9	21.0-28.9	29.0+	
	Million cubic feet										
Softwood:											
Douglas-fir	84	183	403	511	594	614	622	581	1,343	549	5,483
Grand fir	3	6	7	5	14	8	6	7	10	3	69
Noble fir	1	5	9	2	7	12	10	6	18	1	71
Pacific silver fir	—	—	—	—	—	—	—	—	—	—	4
Ponderosa pine	—	—	—	—	1	—	—	—	1	1	4
Sitka spruce	2	9	19	24	34	37	52	31	45	61	313
Western hemlock	61	146	192	273	294	261	134	102	220	62	1,745
Western redcedar	2	8	10	13	17	16	16	31	86	104	302
Total softwoods	154	357	642	828	961	946	840	758	1,722	781	7,988
Hardwood:											
Bigleaf maple	14	26	37	46	37	47	35	39	95	55	432
Black cottonwood	—	1	1	—	2	—	—	5	11	19	39
Black locust	—	—	—	—	—	—	—	—	—	—	—
Cherry	4	3	1	3	2	1	—	—	—	—	14
Oregon ash	—	2	2	3	3	4	1	—	—	1	16
Oregon white oak	6	11	10	18	15	17	21	13	28	6	145
Pacific madrone	—	—	2	1	—	—	—	—	—	—	3
Red alder	69	110	177	182	219	133	88	81	78	9	1,145
White alder	1	—	—	—	—	—	—	—	—	—	1
Total hardwoods	94	153	230	252	277	201	145	137	213	92	1,795
All species	248	510	871	1,080	1,238	1,148	985	894	1,935	873	9,783

— = less than 500,000 cubic feet found.

[a] Totals may be off because of rounding; data subject to sampling error.

Table 9c—Estimated net volume of growing-stock on nonfederal timberland, by species and diameter class, west-central Oregon, January 1, 1997[ab]

Species	Diameter class (inches at breast height)										All classes
	5.0-6.9	7.0-8.9	9.0-10.9	11.0-12.9	13.0-14.9	15.0-16.9	17.0-18.9	19.0-20.9	21.0-28.9	29.0+	
	Million cubic feet										
Softwood:											
Douglas-fir	99	250	356	454	425	440	402	394	861	477	4,158
Grand fir	5	7	9	7	18	8	4	9	22	2	91
Incense-cedar	2	1	2	1	2	—	3	3	5	7	25
Lodgepole pine	—	1	1	6	—	1	2	—	5	3	12
Noble fir	—	—	—	1	—	2	4	—	5	3	16
Ponderosa pine	—	—	1	—	6	2	3	—	2	6	20
Sitka spruce	1	1	3	13	10	26	5	21	46	133	260
Western hemlock	25	53	80	76	108	91	66	49	93	26	668
Western redcedar	2	4	7	5	3	8	3	5	14	10	61
Western white pine	—	—	—	—	—	—	1	—	—	—	1
Total softwoods	135	317	459	563	573	580	494	480	1,047	664	5,313
Hardwood:											
Bigleaf maple	14	16	20	27	21	25	20	22	44	29	238
Black cottonwood	—	—	—	1	—	—	1	—	—	2	5
California black oak	3	1	7	1	1	5	5	4	5	—	32
Cherry	1	1	—	1	—	2	—	—	—	—	5
Golden chinkapin	1	9	16	10	5	—	4	—	—	—	45
Oregon ash	5	2	1	2	2	—	2	2	2	2	19
Oregon white oak	2	3	14	10	8	12	9	6	37	10	110
Pacific madrone	6	2	—	—	—	2	—	—	3	—	13
Red alder	17	39	72	88	49	56	30	15	35	12	414
Total hardwoods	48	75	131	140	86	102	71	48	125	55	881
All species	183	392	590	703	659	682	565	528	1,173	719	6,194

— = less than 500,000 cubic feet found.

[a] Totals may be off because of rounding; data subject to sampling error.

[b] Includes growing-stock trees 5.0 inches in d.b.h. and larger.

Table 9d—Estimated net volume of growing-stock on nonfederal timberland, by species and diameter class, southwest Oregon, January 1, 1997[a][b]

Species	Diameter class (inches at breast height) Million cubic feet										All classes
	5.0-6.9	7.0-8.9	9.0-10.9	11.0-12.9	13.0-14.9	15.0-16.9	17.0-18.9	19.0-20.9	21.0-28.9	29.0+	
Softwood:											
Douglas-fir	177	329	456	527	561	515	402	311	725	592	4,594
Grand fir	15	24	29	24	24	53	35	29	90	20	344
Incense-cedar	17	13	21	5	19	15	12	12	25	18	156
Jeffrey pine	—	1	—	—	1	—	—	—	1	—	2
Knobcone pine	—	—	—	—	—	—	—	—	—	—	1
Lodgepole pine	—	—	—	—	2	1	—	—	—	—	3
Ponderosa pine	6	2	7	9	11	12	8	13	22	24	114
Port-Orford-cedar	4	9	4	7	2	5	6	4	8	2	52
Redwood	—	—	1	1	4	4	2	9	10	4	34
Sitka spruce	4	6	6	4	8	2	8	—	23	27	88
Sugar pine	—	1	3	1	4	3	2	4	5	5	28
Western hemlock	13	18	13	30	40	19	18	24	33	21	228
Western redcedar	2	2	8	4	12	3	5	6	15	70	127
White fir	2	10	14	16	16	17	12	8	12	3	110
Total softwoods	240	414	562	629	703	648	510	422	968	786	5,882
Hardwood:											
Bigleaf maple	7	11	15	15	13	11	21	9	33	31	166
Black cottonwood	—	—	—	—	—	—	—	—	—	2	2
California black oak	12	12	11	14	15	6	12	21	17	19	140
California-laurel	5	8	18	6	6	4	3	4	9	6	70
Canyon live oak	5	3	6	—	5	—	—	—	—	6	19
Cherry	—	1	1	—	—	—	—	—	—	—	2
Golden chinkapin	18	19	7	3	9	—	2	—	—	—	58
Oregon ash	3	1	—	—	2	—	—	—	—	—	7
Oregon white oak	5	9	13	19	25	25	7	5	2	5	118
Pacific madrone	40	49	75	46	39	40	28	11	36	14	379
Red alder	31	60	92	89	81	76	44	36	49	—	557
Tanoak	23	24	14	8	12	8	15	6	21	7	139
Total hardwoods	148	198	252	200	206	171	133	92	172	85	1,657
All species	388	612	814	829	910	819	643	513	1,140	871	7,538

— = less than 500,000 cubic feet found.
[a] Totals may be off because of rounding; data subject to sampling error.
[b] Includes growing-stock trees 5.0 inches in d.b.h. and larger.

Table 10a—Estimated net volume of sawtimber on nonfederal timberland, by species and diameter class, western Oregon, January 1, 1997[a][b]

Species	9.0-10.9	11.0-12.9	13.0-14.9	15.0-16.9	17.0-18.9	19.0-20.9	21.0-28.9	29.0+	All classes
					Million board feet, Scribner rule				
Softwood:									
Douglas-fir	3,086	4,842	5,830	6,325	6,136	5,787	14,124	8,470	54,599
Grand fir	118	123	231	293	197	210	610	136	1,917
Incense-cedar	33	14	44	38	37	40	91	91	389
Jeffrey pine	—	—	—	—	—	1	7	—	8
Knobcone pine	—	—	2	—	—	—	—	—	2
Lodgepole pine	3	17	7	10	9	—	—	—	46
Noble fir	20	11	25	61	60	25	101	19	322
Ponderosa pine	15	23	53	49	40	56	113	175	523
Port-Orford-cedar	7	15	5	13	18	14	28	7	107
Redwood	1	2	10	11	7	34	39	23	128
Sitka spruce	71	123	179	239	259	207	479	1,117	2,673
Sugar pine	5	3	10	11	5	18	21	26	98
Western hemlock	784	1,287	1,709	1,554	976	794	1,642	563	9,310
Western redcedar	63	60	102	93	83	161	456	789	1,807
Western white pine	—	—	—	—	6	—	—	—	6
White fir	29	44	53	56	44	31	46	13	317
Total softwoods	4,235	6,566	8,260	8,753	7,877	7,377	17,756	11,429	72,253
Hardwood:									
Bigleaf maple	—	366	304	358	275	274	688	378	2,643
Black cottonwood	—	3	8	—	5	24	61	139	240
California black oak	—	30	31	19	33	57	54	58	283
California-laurel	—	15	17	12	9	13	31	17	114
Canyon live oak	—	—	12	—	—	—	—	—	12
Cherry	—	15	8	12	—	—	—	—	35
Golden chinkapin	—	39	48	—	23	—	—	—	110
Oregon ash	—	5	11	7	8	2	8	11	51
Oregon white oak	—	108	115	133	90	51	167	50	714
Pacific madrone	—	133	115	132	83	21	99	23	606
Red alder	—	1,319	1,527	1,269	793	683	830	99	6,521
Tanoak	—	23	36	27	51	23	78	31	269
Total hardwoods	—	2,057	2,232	1,968	1,370	1,148	2,017	807	11,599
All species	4,235	8,623	10,491	10,721	9,248	8,525	19,773	12,236	83,852

— = less than 500,000 board feet found.

[a] Totals may be off because of rounding; data subject to sampling error.

[b] Includes softwood sawtimber trees 9.0 inches in d.b.h. and larger, and hardwood sawtimber trees 11.0 inches in d.b.h. and larger.

Table 10b—Estimated net volume of sawtimber on nonfederal timberland, by species and diameter class, northwest Oregon, January 1, 1997[a][b]

Species	Diameter class (inches at breast height)								All classes
	9.0-10.9	11.0-12.9	13.0-14.9	15.0-16.9	17.0-18.9	19.0-20.9	21.0-28.9	29.0+	
	Million board feet, Scribner rule								
Softwood:									
Douglas-fir	1,052	1,689	2,222	2,516	2,724	2,661	6,508	2,860	22,231
Grand fir	20	17	59	34	27	35	43	15	250
Noble fir	20	7	25	51	40	25	81	5	254
Ponderosa pine	—	—	1	—	—	—	7	7	15
Sitka spruce	47	68	117	131	203	121	188	305	1,179
Western hemlock	528	931	1,147	1,106	607	462	1,054	320	6,155
Western redcedar	24	36	55	55	58	122	349	447	1,146
Total softwoods	1,690	2,749	3,626	3,892	3,659	3,426	8,229	3,957	31,229
Hardwood:									
Bigleaf maple	—	192	163	212	128	146	430	203	1,474
Black cottonwood	—	—	8	—	—	24	61	114	207
Cherry	—	10	8	5	—	—	—	—	23
Oregon ash	—	3	5	7	3	—	—	5	24
Oregon white oak	—	41	35	40	49	32	66	16	278
Pacific madrone	—	3	—	—	—	—	—	—	3
Red alder	—	667	961	639	429	419	407	42	3,564
Total hardwoods	—	917	1,181	902	608	621	964	381	5,574
All species	1,690	3,666	4,806	4,794	4,267	4,047	9,193	4,338	36,802

— = less than 500,000 board feet found.

[a] Totals may be off because of rounding; data subject to sampling error.

[b] Includes softwood sawtimber trees 9.0 inches in d.b.h. and larger, and hardwood sawtimber trees 11.0 inches in d.b.h. and larger.

Table 10c—Estimated net volume of sawtimber on nonfederal timberland, by species and diameter class, west-central Oregon, January 1, 1997[a][b]

Species	9.0-10.9	11.0-12.9	13.0-14.9	15.0-16.9	17.0-18.9	19.0-20.9	21.0-28.9	29.0+	All classes
				Million board feet, Scribner rule					
Softwood:									
Douglas-fir	899	1,484	1,595	1,800	1,739	1,784	4,178	2,476	15,955
Grand fir	26	24	76	34	19	40	103	9	332
Incense-cedar	3	3	5	—	8	7	13	24	64
Lodgepole pine	3	17	—	5	9	—	—	—	34
Noble fir	—	4	—	10	20	—	20	14	68
Ponderosa pine	2	—	19	8	10	—	8	30	77
Sitka spruce	7	44	36	102	19	86	187	677	1,158
Western hemlock	225	252	416	376	292	225	441	133	2,360
Western redcedar	17	14	7	30	10	17	50	38	183
Western white pine	—	—	—	—	6	—	—	—	6
Total softwoods	1,183	1,842	2,153	2,365	2,131	2,159	5,002	3,401	20,235
Hardwood:									
Bigleaf maple	—	114	90	116	72	97	164	79	731
Black cottonwood	—	3	—	—	5	—	—	12	20
California black oak	—	2	3	9	11	9	14	—	48
Cherry	—	5	—	7	—	—	—	—	12
Golden chinkapin	—	30	20	—	17	—	—	—	67
Oregon ash	—	1	3	—	5	2	6	6	24
Oregon white oak	—	26	19	31	23	8	88	24	219
Pacific madrone	—	—	—	10	—	—	11	—	21
Red alder	—	328	217	266	142	71	169	57	1,249
Total hardwoods	—	509	353	438	276	186	452	178	2,392
All species	1,183	2,351	2,506	2,803	2,407	2,345	5,454	3,579	22,627

— = less than 500,000 board feet found.

[a] Totals may be off because of rounding; data subject to sampling error.

[b] Includes softwood sawtimber trees 9.0 inches in d.b.h. and larger, and hardwood sawtimber trees 11.0 inches in d.b.h. and larger

Table 10d—Estimated net volume of sawtimber on nonfederal timberland, by species and diameter class, southwest Oregon, January 1, 1997[a][b]

Species	Diameter class (inches at breast height								All classes
	9.0-10.9	11.0-12.9	13.0-14.9	15.0-16.9	17.0-18.9	19.0-20.9	21.0-28.9	29.0+	
	Million board feet, Scribner rule								
Softwood:									
Douglas-fir	1,136	1,668	2,013	2,010	1,674	1,341	3,438	3,134	16,413
Grand fir	71	81	96	224	151	135	464	112	1,335
Incense-cedar	31	10	39	38	29	33	77	67	325
Jeffrey pine	—	—	—	—	—	1	7	—	8
Knobcone pine	—	—	2	—	—	—	—	—	2
Lodgepole pine	—	—	7	6	—	—	—	—	12
Ponderosa pine	13	23	33	41	30	56	98	138	432
Port-Orford-cedar	7	15	5	13	18	14	28	7	107
Redwood	1	2	10	11	7	34	39	23	128
Sitka spruce	17	11	26	6	36	—	104	135	336
Sugar pine	5	3	10	11	5	18	21	26	98
Western hemlock	31	104	146	73	77	107	146	111	796
Western redcedar	21	11	40	8	15	22	57	304	478
White fir	29	44	53	56	44	31	46	13	317
Total softwoods	1,362	1,975	2,481	2,496	2,087	1,792	4,525	4,071	20,789
Hardwood:									
Bigleaf maple	—	60	51	31	75	31	94	97	438
Black cottonwood	—	—	—	—	—	—	—	13	13
California black oak	—	28	28	10	22	48	40	58	234
California-laurel	—	15	17	12	9	13	31	17	114
Canyon live oak	—	—	12	—	—	—	—	—	12
Golden chinkapin	—	9	27	—	6	—	—	—	42
Oregon ash	—	—	2	—	—	—	2	—	4
Oregon white oak	—	41	61	62	18	11	13	9	217
Pacific madrone	—	130	115	122	83	21	88	23	582
Red alder	—	324	349	365	222	194	255	—	1,708
Tanoak	—	23	36	27	51	23	78	31	269
Total hardwoods	—	631	699	628	487	341	601	248	3,634
All species	1,362	2,606	3,180	3,124	2,573	2,133	5,126	4,319	24,423

— = less than 500,000 board feet found.

[a] Totals may be off because of rounding; data subject to sampling error.

[b] Includes softwood sawtimber trees 9.0 inches in d.b.h. and larger, and hardwood sawtimber trees 11.0 inches in d.b.h. and larger.

Table 11a—Estimated net volume of growing-stock and sawtimber on nonfederal timberland, by class of timber, owner class, and species group, western Oregon, January 1, 1997[a]

Class of timber and owner class	Average volume	Species group		All species
		Softwoods	Hardwoods	
	Cubic feet per acre	*– – – – – Million cubic feet – – – – –*		
Growing-stock:[b]				
Other public	5,160	3,683	703	4,386
Forest industry	3,235	11,483	2,038	13,521
Other private	2,983	4,017	1,591	5,608
Total, growing-stock	3,404	19,183	4,332	23,515
	Board feet per acre	*– – – – – Million cubic feet – – – – –*		
Sawtimber (Scribner rule):[c]				
Other public	20,587	15,276	2,223	17,499
Forest industry	11,169	41,679	4,995	46,674
Other private	10,468	15,299	4,381	19,680
Total, sawtimber	12,137	72,253	11,599	83,852

[a] Totals may be off because of rounding; data subject to sampling error.

[b] Includes growing-stock trees 5.0 inches in d.b.h. and larger.

[c] Includes softwood sawtimber trees 9.0 inches in d.b.h. and larger and hardwood sawtimber trees 11.0 inches in d.b.h. and larger.

Table 11b—Estimated net volume of growing-stock and sawtimber on nonfederal timberland, by class of timber, owner class, and species group, northwest Oregon, January 1, 1997[a]

Class of timber and owner class	Average volume	Species group		All species
		Softwoods	Hardwoods	
	Cubic feet per acre	----- *Million cubic feet* -----		
Growing-stock:[b]				
Other public	5,348	2,538	537	3,075
Forest industry	4,090	3,987	527	4,515
Other private	3,175	1,463	731	2,194
Total, growing-stock	4,131	7,988	2,194	9,783
	Board feet per acre	----- *Million cubic feet* -----		
Sawtimber (Scribner rule):[c]				
Other public	20,524	10,089	1,692	11,781
Forest industry	14,888	14,968	1,468	16,436
Other private	12,424	6,171	2,414	8,585
Total, sawtimber	15,541	31,229	5,574	36,802

[a] Totals may be off because of rounding; data subject to sampling error.

[b] Includes growing-stock trees 5.0 inches in d.b.h. and larger.

[c] Includes softwood sawtimber trees 9.0 inches in d.b.h. and larger and hardwood sawtimber trees 11.0 inches in d.b.h. and larger

Table 11c—Estimated net volume of growing-stock and sawtimber on nonfederal timberland, by class of timber, owner class, and species group, west-central Oregon, January 1, 1997[a]

Class of timber and owner class	Average volume	Species group		All species
		Softwoods	Hardwoods	
	Cubic feet per acre	– – – – – *Million cubic feet* – – – – –		
Growing-stock:[b]				
Other public	4,237	363	48	411
Forest industry	3,272	3,902	481	4,382
Other private	3,256	1,048	352	1,400
Total, growing-stock	3,318	5,313	881	6,194
	Board feet per acre	– – – – – *Million cubic feet* – – – – –		
Sawtimber (Scribner rule):[c]				
Other public	19,062	1,692	157	1,849
Forest industry	11,780	14,545	1,228	15,773
Other private	11,642	3,999	1,007	5,006
Total, sawtimber	12,119	20,235	2,392	22,627

[a] Totals may be off because of rounding; data subject to sampling error.

[b] Includes growing-stock trees 5.0 inches in d.b.h. and larger.

[c] Includes softwood sawtimber trees 9.0 inches in d.b.h. and larger and hardwood sawtimber trees 11.0 inches in d.b.h. and larger.

Table 11d—Estimated net volume of growing-stock and sawtimber on nonfederal timberland, by class of timber, owner class, and species group, southwest Oregon, January 1, 1997[a]

Class of timber and owner class	Average volume	Species group		All species
		Softwoods	Hardwoods	
	Cubic feet per acre	– – – – – *Million cubic feet* – – – – –		
Growing-stock:[b]				
Other public	5,028	783	117	900
Forest industry	2,664	3,594	1,031	4,625
Other private	2,068	1,142	427	1,570
Total, growing-stock	2,684	5,882	1,657	7,538
	Board feet per acre	– – – – –*Million cubic feet*– – – – –		
Sawtimber (Scribner rule):[c]				
Other public	21,614	3,495	374	3,869
Forest industry	8,332	12,166	2,299	14,465
Other private	8,023	5,129	961	6,090
Total, sawtimber	8,694	20,789	3,634	24,423

[a] Totals may be off because of rounding; data subject to sampling error.

[b] Includes growing-stock trees 5.0 inches in d.b.h. and larger.

[c] Includes softwood sawtimber trees 9.0 inches in d.b.h. and larger and hardwood sawtimber trees 11.0 inches in d.b.h. and larger.

Table 12a—Estimated net volume of growing-stock on nonfederal timberland, by species and owner class, western Oregon, January 1, 1997[a b]

Species	Other public	Forest industry	Other private	All owners
	Million cubic feet			
Softwood:				
Douglas-fir	2,881	8,244	3,111	14,235
Grand fir	33	297	175	505
Incense-cedar	9	101	72	182
Jeffrey pine	—	2	—	2
Knobcone pine	—	1	—	1
Lodgepole pine	—	—	15	15
Noble fir	27	60	—	87
Ponderosa pine	8	38	91	138
Port-Orford-cedar	4	31	16	52
Redwood	—	31	3	34
Sitka spruce	81	436	145	662
Sugar pine	4	16	8	28
Western hemlock	582	1,915	144	2,641
Western redcedar	40	238	212	490
Western white pine	—	—	1	1
White fir	13	73	24	110
Total	3,683	11,483	4,017	19,183
Hardwood:				
Bigleaf maple	107	357	372	836
Black cottonwood	5	15	26	45
California black oak	9	37	126	171
California-laurel	7	55	9	70
Canyon live oak	1	14	4	19
Cherry	1	8	12	20
Golden chinkapin	—	94	10	103
Oregon ash	—	17	25	42
Oregon white oak	10	150	213	373
Pacific madrone	26	197	172	395
Red alder	537	986	594	2,117
Tanoak	1	108	30	139
Total	703	2,038	1,591	4,332
All species	4,386	13,521	5,608	23,515

— = less than 500,000 cubic feet found.
[a] Totals may be off because of rounding; data subject to sampling error.
[b] Includes growing-stock trees 5 inches in d.b.h. and larger.

Table 12b—Estimated net volume of growing-stock on nonfederal timberland, by species and owner class, northwest Oregon, January 1, 1997[a][b]

Species	Other public	Forest industry	Other private	All owners
	Million cubic feet			
Softwood:				
Douglas-fir	1,844	2,490	1,149	5,483
Grand fir	22	22	25	69
Noble fir	27	44	—	71
Ponderosa pine	—	3	1	4
Sitka spruce	52	222	39	313
Western hemlock	555	1,124	66	1,745
Western redcedar	38	82	182	302
Total	2,538	3,987	1,463	7,988
Hardwood:				
Bigleaf maple	90	103	239	432
Black cottonwood	—	15	24	39
Cherry	1	4	8	14
Oregon ash	—	1	15	16
Oregon white oak	—	19	125	145
Pacific madrone	3	—	—	3
Red alder	442	383	320	1,145
Total	537	527	731	1,795
All species	3,075	4,514	2,194	9,783

— = less than 500,000 cubic feet found.

[a] Totals may be off because of rounding; data subject to sampling error.

[b] Includes growing-stock trees 5 inches in d.b.h. and larger.

Table 12c—Estimated net volume of growing-stock on nonfederal timberland, by species and owner class, west-central Oregon, January 1, 1997[a][b]

Species	Other public	Forest industry	Other private	All owners
	Million cubic feet			
Softwood:				
Douglas-fir	359	2,978	822	4,158
Grand fir	—	37	54	91
Incense-cedar	—	21	4	25
Lodgepole pine	—	—	12	12
Noble fir	—	16	—	16
Ponderosa pine	—	1	19	20
Sitka spruce	—	187	73	260
Western hemlock	5	612	51	668
Western redcedar	—	48	12	61
Western white pine	—	—	1	1
Total	363	3,902	1,048	5,313
Hardwood:				
Bigleaf maple	9	131	98	238
Black cottonwood	5	—	—	5
California black oak	—	—	32	32
Cherry	—	1	3	5
Golden chinkapin	—	39	6	45
Oregon ash	—	12	7	19
Oregon white oak	—	74	36	110
Pacific madrone	—	7	7	13
Red alder	35	217	163	414
Total	48	481	352	881
All species	411	4,382	1,400	6,194

— = less than 500,000 cubic feet found.

[a] Totals may be off because of rounding; data subject to sampling error.

[b] Includes growing-stock trees 5 inches in d.b.h. and larger.

Table 12d—Estimated net volume of growing-stock on nonfederal timberland, by species and owner class, southwest Oregon, January 1, 1997[a][b]

Species	Other public	Forest industry	Other private	All owners
	Million cubic feet			
Softwood:				
Douglas-fir	679	2,775	1,140	4,594
Grand fir	11	238	96	344
Incense-cedar	9	80	67	156
Jeffrey pine	—	2	—	2
Knobcone pine	—	1	—	1
Lodgepole pine	—	—	3	3
Ponderosa pine	8	34	71	114
Port-Orford-cedar	4	31	16	52
Redwood	—	31	3	34
Sitka spruce	29	26	33	88
Sugar pine	4	16	8	28
Western hemlock	23	179	27	228
Western redcedar	2	107	18	127
White fir	13	73	24	110
Total	783	3,594	1,505	5,882
Hardwood:				
Bigleaf maple	7	123	35	166
Black cottonwood	—	—	2	2
California black oak	9	37	94	140
California-laurel	7	55	9	70
Canyon live oak	1	14	4	19
Cherry	—	2	—	2
Golden chinkapin	—	54	4	58
Oregon ash	—	4	2	7
Oregon white oak	10	57	51	118
Pacific madrone	23	190	165	379
Red alder	60	386	112	557
Tanoak	1	108	30	139
Total	117	1,031	508	1,657
All species	900	4,625	2,014	7,538

— = less than 500,000 cubic feet found.

[a] Totals may be off because of rounding; data subject to sampling error.

[b] Includes growing-stock trees 5 inches in d.b.h. and larger.

Table 13a—Estimated net volume of sawtimber on nonfederal timberland, by species and owner class, western Oregon, January 1, 1997[a][b]

Species	Other public	Forest industry	Other private	All owners
	Million board feet, Scribner rule			
Softwood:				
Douglas-fir	12,195	30,384	12,020	54,599
Grand fir	107	1,150	660	1,917
Incense-cedar	32	227	130	389
Jeffrey pine	—	7	1	8
Knobcone pine	—	2	—	2
Lodgepole pine	—	—	46	46
Noble fir	102	220	—	322
Ponderosa pine	41	145	337	523
Port-Orford-cedar	13	58	36	107
Redwood	—	123	5	128
Sitka spruce	285	1,767	620	2,673
Sugar pine	11	59	29	98
Western hemlock	2,295	6,492	523	9,310
Western redcedar	147	856	804	1,807
Western white pine	—	—	6	6
White fir	48	188	82	317
Total	15,276	41,679	15,299	72,253
Hardwood:				
Bigleaf maple	385	1,057	1,202	2,643
Black cottonwood	20	77	142	240
California black oak	13	67	203	283
California-laurel	11	86	17	114
Canyon live oak	—	12	1	12
Cherry	—	—	35	35
Golden chinkapin	—	101	9	110
Oregon ash	—	5	46	51
Oregon white oak	23	319	371	714
Pacific madrone	39	301	267	606
Red alder	1,731	2,762	2,028	6,521
Tanoak	—	209	60	269
Total	2,223	4,995	4,381	11,599
All species	17,499	46,674	19,680	83,852

— = less than 500,000 board feet found.

[a] Totals may be off because of rounding; data subject to sampling error.

[b] Includes softwood sawtimber trees 9.0 inches in d.b.h. and larger and hardwood sawtimber trees 11.0 inches in d.b.h. and larger.

Table 13b—Estimated net volume of sawtimber on nonfederal timberland, by species and owner class, northwest Oregon, January 1, 1997[a][b]

Species	Other public	Forest industry	Other private	All owners
	Million board feet, Scribner rule			
Softwood:				
Douglas-fir	7,372	9,925	4,934	22,231
Grand fir	83	77	90	250
Noble fir	102	152	—	254
Ponderosa pine	—	8	7	15
Sitka spruce	188	813	178	1,179
Western hemlock	2,204	3,700	250	6,155
Western redcedar	140	293	712	1,146
Total	10,089	14,968	6,171	31,229
Hardwood:				
Bigleaf maple	320	345	810	1,474
Black cottonwood	—	77	130	207
Cherry	—	—	23	23
Oregon ash	—	—	24	24
Oregon white oak	—	38	241	278
Pacific madrone	3	—	—	3
Red alder	1,369	1,008	1,187	3,564
Total	1,692	1,468	2,414	5,574
All species	11,781	16,436	8,585	36,802

— = less than 500,000 board feet found.

[a] Totals may be off because of rounding; data subject to sampling error.

[b] Includes softwood sawtimber trees 9.0 inches in d.b.h. and larger and hardwood sawtimber trees 11.0 inches in d.b.h. and larger.

Table 13c—Estimated net volume of sawtimber on nonfederal timberland, by species and owner class, west-central Oregon, January 1, 1997[a][b]

Species	Other public	Forest industry	Other private	All owners
	Million board feet, Scribner rule			
Softwood:				
Douglas-fir	1,676	11,120	3,159	15,955
Grand fir	—	119	212	332
Incense-cedar	—	56	7	64
Lodgepole pine	—	—	34	34
Noble fir	—	68	—	68
Ponderosa pine	—	4	73	77
Sitka spruce	—	853	306	1,158
Western hemlock	16	2,180	164	2,360
Western redcedar	—	144	39	183
Western white pine	—	—	6	6
Total	1,692	14,545	3,999	20,235
Hardwood:				
Bigleaf maple	44	389	298	731
Black cottonwood	20	—	—	20
California black oak	—	—	48	48
Cherry	—	—	12	12
Golden chinkapin	—	63	4	67
Oregon ash	—	3	20	24
Oregon white oak	—	158	61	219
Pacific madrone	—	17	5	21
Red alder	92	598	558	1,249
Total	157	1,228	1,007	2,392
All species	1,849	15,773	5,006	22,627

— = less than 500,000 board feet found.

[a] Totals may be off because of rounding; data subject to sampling error.

[b] Includes softwood sawtimber trees 9.0 inches in d.b.h. and larger and hardwood sawtimber trees 11.0 inches in d.b.h. and larger.

Table 13d—Estimated net volume of sawtimber on nonfederal timberland, by species and owner class, southwest Oregon, January 1, 1997[a][b]

Species	Other public	Forest industry	Other private	All owners
	Million board feet, Scribner rule			
Softwood:				
Douglas-fir	3,147	9,339	3,927	16,413
Grand fir	24	954	358	1,335
Incense-cedar	32	171	122	325
Jeffrey pine	—	7	1	8
Knobcone pine	—	2	—	2
Lodgepole pine	—	—	12	12
Ponderosa pine	41	133	258	432
Port-Orford-cedar	13	58	36	107
Redwood	—	123	5	128
Sitka spruce	98	102	137	336
Sugar pine	11	59	29	98
Western hemlock	75	612	109	796
Western redcedar	7	419	52	478
White fir	48	188	82	317
Total	3,495	12,166	5,129	20,789
Hardwood:				
Bigleaf maple	21	323	93	438
Black cottonwood	—	—	13	13
California black oak	13	67	155	234
California-laurel	11	86	17	114
Canyon live oak	—	12	1	12
Golden chinkapin	—	38	5	42
Oregon ash	—	2	2	4
Oregon white oak	23	123	70	217
Pacific madrone	36	284	262	582
Red alder	269	1,155	283	1,708
Tanoak	—	209	60	269
Total	374	2,299	961	3,634
All species	3,869	14,465	6,090	24,423

— = less than 500,000 board feet found.

[a] Totals may be off because of rounding; data subject to sampling error.

[b] Includes softwood sawtimber trees 9.0 inches in d.b.h. and larger and hardwood sawtimber trees 11.0 inches in d.b.h. and larger.

Table 14a—Estimated net volume of growing-stock on nonfederal timberland, by forest type and stand-size class, western Oregon, January 1, 1997[a b]

Forest type	Large sawtimber	Small sawtimber	Pole-timber	Seedling-sapling	All classes
	Million cubic feet				
Softwood:					
Douglas-fir	2,039	11,796	802	399	15,035
Grand fir	70	99	—	59	227
Incense-cedar	24	30	70	19	143
Noble fir	—	8	8	1	17
Pacific silver fir	—	—	—	2	2
Ponderosa pine	—	52	—	6	58
Port-Orford-cedar	—	—	24	—	24
Redwood	—	38	—	—	38
Sitka spruce	252	281	9	3	544
Western hemlock	6	1,887	142	45	2,080
Western redcedar	199	103	—	3	305
White fir	4	57	—	8	69
Total	2,593	14,351	1,054	546	18,544
Hardwood:					
Apple	—	—	3	2	5
Bigleaf maple	63	263	100	16	441
Black cottonwood	—	16	—	7	24
California black oak	—	60	31	—	91
California-laurel	—	107	16	—	122
Canyon live oak	—	—	22	9	31
Cherry	—	—	2	3	5
Oregon ash	11	3	—	9	23
Oregon white oak	1	273	68	40	382
Pacific madrone	—	107	307	54	468
Red alder	71	1,857	593	74	2,594
Tanoak	25	118	96	22	261
Willow	—	—	—	3	3
Total	171	2,802	1,237	239	4,449
Nonstocked[c]	—	—	—	—	522
All types	2,764	17,154	2,291	784	23,515

— = less than 500,000 cubic feet found.

[a] Totals may be off because of rounding; data subject to sampling error.

[b] Includes growing-stock trees 5 inches in d.b.h. and larger.

[c] Nonstocked areas are less than 10 percent stocked with live trees. Includes projected access-denied areas.

Table 14b—Estimated net volume of growing-stock on nonfederal timberland, by forest type and stand-size class, northwest Oregon, January 1, 1997[a][b]

Forest type	Large sawtimber	Small sawtimber	Pole-timber	Seedling-sapling	All classes
	Million cubic feet				
Softwoods:					
Douglas-fir	843	4,567	115	103	5,628
Grand fir	—	21	—	—	21
Noble fir	—	8	8	—	16
Pacific silver fir	—	—	—	2	2
Sitka spruce	14	200	9	3	224
Western hemlock	6	1,404	105	27	1,542
Western redcedar	193	25	—	3	222
Total	1,056	6,226	236	137	7,655
Hardwood:					
Apple	—	—	3	—	3
Bigleaf maple	47	223	12	15	298
Black cottonwood	—	16	—	7	24
Cherry	—	—	2	3	5
Oregon ash	—	3	—	—	3
Oregon white oak	1	63	41	14	119
Red alder	37	1,084	176	33	1,330
Total	85	1,389	234	72	1,780
Nonstocked[c]	—	—	—	—	347
All types	1,141	7,614	470	210	9,783

— = less than 500,000 cubic feet found.

[a] Totals may be off because of rounding; data subject to sampling error.

[b] Includes growing-stock trees 5 inches in d.b.h. and larger.

[c] Nonstocked areas are less than 10 percent stocked with live trees. Includes projected access-denied areas.

Table 14c—Estimated net volume of growing-stock on nonfederal timberland, by forest type and stand-size class, west-central Oregon, January 1, 1997[a][b]

Forest type	Large sawtimber	Small sawtimber	Pole-timber	Seedling-sapling	All classes
	Million cubic feet				
Softwoods:					
Douglas-fir	467	3,620	265	108	4,460
Grand fir	—	36	—	39	75
Incense-cedar	18	—	—	—	18
Noble fir	—	—	—	1	1
Ponderosa pine	—	6	—	—	6
Sitka spruce	204	60	—	—	264
Western hemlock	—	453	15	12	480
Western redcedar	6	2	—	—	8
Total	695	4,178	280	160	5,313
Hardwood:					
Bigleaf maple	16	18	48	—	82
California black oak	—	21	—	—	21
Oregon ash	11	—	—	9	20
Oregon white oak	—	120	16	7	143
Pacific madrone	—	—	—	5	5
Red alder	—	292	145	9	445
Total	27	450	209	30	717
Nonstocked[c]	—	—	—	—	164
All types	722	4,628	490	189	6,194

— = less than 500,000 cubic feet found.

[a] Totals may be off because of rounding; data subject to sampling error.

[b] Includes growing-stock trees 5 inches in d.b.h. and larger.

[c] Nonstocked areas are less than 10 percent stocked with live trees. Includes projected access-denied areas.

Table 14d—Estimated net volume of growing-stock on nonfederal timberland, by forest type and stand-size class, southwest Oregon, January 1, 1997[a][b]

Forest type	Large sawtimber	Small sawtimber	Pole-timber	Seedling-sapling	All classes
	Million cubic feet				
Softwoods:					
Douglas-fir	728	3,609	422	188	4,947
Grand fir	70	42	—	20	131
Incense-cedar	6	30	70	19	125
Ponderosa pine	—	46	—	6	52
Port-Orford-cedar	—	—	24	—	24
Redwood	—	38	—	—	38
Sitka spruce	34	21	—	1	56
Western hemlock	—	30	21	7	59
Western redcedar	—	75	—	—	75
White fir	4	57	—	8	69
Total	842	3,948	537	249	5,576
Hardwood:					
Apple	—	—	—	2	2
Bigleaf maple	—	22	39	—	61
California black oak	—	39	31	—	70
California-laurel	—	107	16	—	122
Canyon live oak	—	—	22	9	31
Oregon white oak	—	90	11	19	119
Pacific madrone	—	107	307	49	464
Red alder	33	481	273	32	819
Tanoak	25	118	96	22	261
Willow	—	—	—	3	3
Total	58	963	794	137	1,952
Nonstocked[c]	—	—	—	—	10
All types	900	4,911	1,331	386	7,538

— = less than 500,000 cubic feet found.

[a] Totals may be off because of rounding; data subject to sampling error.

[b] Includes growing-stock trees 5 inches in d.b.h. and larger.

[c] Nonstocked areas are less than 10 percent stocked with live trees.

Table 15a—Estimated net volume of sawtimber on nonfederal timberland, by forest type and stand-size class, western Oregon, January 1, 1997[a][b]

Forest type	Large sawtimber	Small sawtimber	Pole-timber	Seedling-sapling	All classes
	Million board feet, Scribner rule				
Softwoods:					
Douglas-fir	10,047	43,308	1,309	988	55,651
Grand fir	352	343	—	117	812
Incense-cedar	54	100	144	20	318
Jeffrey pine	—	1	—	—	1
Noble fir	—	18	5	—	23
Pacific silver fir	—	—	—	2	2
Ponderosa pine	—	172	—	14	186
Port-Orford-cedar	—	—	39	—	39
Redwood	—	148	—	—	148
Sitka spruce	1,169	910	44	1	2,125
Western hemlock	32	6,983	323	115	7,453
Western redcedar	821	326	—	2	1,149
White fir	17	158	—	17	192
Total	12,492	52,468	1,864	1,276	68,099
Hardwood:					
Apple	—	—	7	7	14
Bigleaf maple	216	946	290	42	1,494
Black cottonwood	—	75	—	29	104
California black oak	—	158	52	—	211
California-laurel	—	342	47	—	389
Canyon live oak	—	—	87	28	115
Cherry	—	—	2	7	9
Oregon ash	39	4	—	36	78
Oregon white oak	3	749	139	80	970
Pacific madrone	—	252	540	62	854
Red alder	337	7,084	1,437	210	9,068
Tanoak	91	345	174	37	646
Willow	—	—	—	6	6
Total	685	9,956	2,775	543	13,958
Nonstocked[c]	—	—	—	—	1,795
All types	13,177	62,424	4,639	1,818	83,852

— = less than 500,000 board feet found.

[a] Totals may be off because of rounding; data subject to sampling error.

[b] Includes softwood sawtimber trees 9.0 inches in d.b.h. and larger and hardwood sawtimber trees 11.0 inches in d.b.h. and larger.

[c] Nonstocked areas are less than 10 percent stocked with live trees. Includes projected access denied areas.

Table 15b—Estimated net volume of sawtimber on nonfederal timberland, by forest type and stand-size class, northwest Oregon, January 1, 1997[a] [b]

Forest type	Large sawtimber	Small sawtimber	Pole-timber	Seedling-sapling	All classes
	Million board feet, Scribner rule				
Softwoods:					
Douglas-fir	4,125	17,489	155	335	22,104
Grand fir	—	57	—	—	57
Noble fir	—	18	5	—	23
Pacific silver fir	—	—	—	2	2
Sitka spruce	69	646	44	—	758
Western hemlock	32	5,123	226	92	5,472
Western redcedar	795	91	—	2	889
Total	5,022	23,424	430	430	29,306
Hardwood:					
Apple	—	—	7	—	7
Bigleaf maple	192	831	40	42	1,105
Black cottonwood	—	75	—	29	104
Cherry	—	—	2	7	9
Oregon ash	—	4	—	—	4
Oregon white oak	3	178	73	40	294
Red alder	168	4,136	372	118	4,794
Total	363	5,224	495	236	6,318
Nonstocked[c]	—	—	—	—	1,179
All types	5,384	28,649	924	667	36,802

— = less than 500,000 board feet found.

[a] Totals may be off because of rounding; data subject to sampling error.

[b] Includes softwood sawtimber trees 9.0 inches in d.b.h. and larger and hardwood sawtimber trees 11.0 inches in d.b.h. and larger.

[c] Nonstocked areas are less than 10 percent stocked with live trees. Includes projected access-denied areas.

Table 15c—Estimated net volume of sawtimber on nonfederal timberland , by forest type and stand-size class, west-central Oregon, January 1, 1997[a][b]

Forest type	Large sawtimber	Small sawtimber	Pole-timber	Seedling-sapling	All classes
	Million board feet, Scribner rule				
Softwoods:					
Douglas-fir	2,318	13,559	458	252	16,587
Grand fir	—	129	—	65	193
Incense-cedar	38	—	—	—	38
Ponderosa pine	—	20	—	—	20
Sitka spruce	959	183	—	—	1,142
Western hemlock	—	1,766	25	5	1,796
Western redcedar	26	7	—	—	33
Total	3,341	15,663	483	322	19,809
Hardwood:					
Bigleaf maple	25	65	133	—	222
California black oak	—	36	—	—	36
Oregon ash	39	—	—	36	74
Oregon white oak	—	305	42	20	367
Pacific madrone	—	—	—	9	9
Red alder	—	1,106	405	10	1,521
Total	63	1,512	580	74	2,230
Nonstocked[c]	—	—	—	—	588
All types	3,404	17,176	1,063	396	22,627

— = less than 500,000 board feet found.

[a] Totals may be off because of rounding; data subject to sampling error.

[b] Includes softwood sawtimber trees 9.0 inches in d.b.h. and larger and hardwood sawtimber trees 11.0 inches in d.b.h. and larger.

[c] Nonstocked areas are less than 10 percent stocked with live trees. Includes projected access-denied areas.

Table 15d—Estimated net volume of sawtimber on nonfederal timberland, by forest type and stand-size class, southwest Oregon, January 1, 1997[a][b]

Forest type	Large sawtimber	Small sawtimber	Pole-timber	Seedling-sapling	All classes
	Million board feet, Scribner rule				
Softwoods:					
Douglas-fir	3,603	12,260	696	401	16,960
Grand fir	352	157	—	52	561
Incense-cedar	16	100	144	20	280
Jeffrey pine	—	1	—	—	1
Ponderosa pine	—	152	—	14	166
Port-Orford-cedar	—	—	39	—	39
Redwood	—	148	—	—	148
Sitka spruce	141	82	—	1	224
Western hemlock	—	95	72	18	185
Western redcedar	—	227	—	—	227
White fir	17	158	—	17	192
Total	4,129	13,381	952	524	18,985
Hardwood:					
Apple	—	—	—	7	7
Bigleaf maple	—	50	117	—	167
California black oak	—	122	52	—	174
California-laurel	—	342	47	—	389
Canyon live oak	—	—	87	28	115
Oregon white oak	—	266	24	19	309
Pacific madrone	—	252	540	53	844
Red alder	168	1,842	660	83	2,753
Tanoak	91	345	174	37	646
Willow	—	—	—	6	6
Total	259	3,219	1,700	232	5,411
Nonstocked[c]	—	—	—	—	28
All types	4,388	16,600	2,652	756	24,423

— = less than 500,000 board feet found.
[a] Totals may be off because of rounding; data subject to sampling error.
[b] Includes softwood sawtimber trees 9.0 inches in d.b.h. and larger and hardwood sawtimber trees 11.0 inches in d.b.h. and larger.
[c] Nonstocked areas are less than 10 percent stocked with live trees.

Table 16a—Estimated net volume of growing-stock on nonfederal timberland, by forest type and owner class, western Oregon, January 1, 1997[a][b]

Forest type	Other public	Forest industry	Other private	All owners
	Million cubic feet			
Softwood:				
Douglas-fir	3,135	8,577	3,323	15,035
Grand fir	—	139	88	227
Incense-cedar	—	87	56	143
Noble fir	8	9	—	17
Pacific silver fir	—	2	—	2
Ponderosa pine	—	9	49	58
Port-Orford-cedar	—	17	7	24
Redwood	—	38	—	38
Sitka spruce	29	364	151	544
Western hemlock	443	1,572	66	2,080
Western redcedar	32	128	146	305
White fir	—	56	13	69
Total	3,648	10,995	3,900	18,544
Hardwood:				
Apple	—	2	3	5
Bigleaf maple	70	150	221	441
Black cottonwood	—	16	7	24
California black oak	—	4	86	91
California-laurel	—	122	—	122
Canyon live oak	—	31	—	31
Cherry	2	—	3	5
Oregon ash	—	—	23	23
Oregon white oak	—	216	166	382
Pacific madrone	45	229	194	468
Red alder	621	1,180	794	2,594
Tanoak	—	190	71	261
Willow	—	—	3	3
Total	738	2,141	1,570	4,449
Nonstocked[c]	—	8	60	69
Unclassified[d]	—	376	77	453
All types	4,386	13,521	5,608	23,515

— = less than 500,000 cubic feet found.

[a] Totals may be off because of rounding; data subject to sampling error.

[b] Includes growing-stock trees 5 inches in d.b.h. and larger.

[c] Nonstocked areas are less than 10 percent stocked with live trees.

[d] Includes volume from access-denied project areas.

Table 16b—Estimated net volume of growing-stock on nonfederal timberland, by forest type and owner class, northwest Oregon, January 1, 1997[a][b]

Forest type	Other public	Forest industry	Other private	All owners
	Million cubic feet			
Softwood:				
Douglas-fir	1,971	2,479	1,178	5,628
Grand fir	—	—	21	21
Noble fir	8	8	—	16
Pacific silver fir	—	2	—	2
Sitka spruce	29	178	18	224
Western hemlock	443	1,064	35	1,542
Western redcedar	32	72	117	222
Total	2,484	3,802	1,369	7,655
Hardwood:				
Apple	—	—	3	3
Bigleaf maple	70	50	178	298
Black cottonwood	—	16	7	24
Cherry	2	—	3	5
Oregon ash	—	—	3	3
Oregon white oak	—	2	117	119
Red alder	519	352	459	1,330
Total	591	420	769	1,780
Nonstocked[c]	—	7	38	45
Unclassified[d]	—	285	18	303
All types	3,075	4,514	2,194	9,783

— = less than 500,000 cubic feet found.

[a] Totals may be off because of rounding; data subject to sampling error.

[b] Includes growing-stock trees 5 inches in d.b.h. and larger.

[c] Nonstocked areas are less than 10 percent stocked with live trees.

[d] Includes volume from access-denied project areas.

Table 16c—Estimated net volume of growing-stock on nonfederal timberland, by forest type and owner class, west-central Oregon, January 1, 1997[a][b]

Forest type	Other public	Forest industry	Other private	All owners
	Million cubic feet			
Softwoods:				
Douglas-fir	380	3,194	886	4,460
Grand fir	—	59	16	75
Incense-cedar	—	18	—	18
Noble fir	—	1	—	1
Ponderosa pine	—	—	6	6
Sitka spruce	—	165	99	264
Western hemlock	—	449	31	480
Western redcedar	—	6	2	8
Total	380	3,892	1,041	5,313
Hardwood:				
Bigleaf maple	—	40	42	82
California black oak	—	—	21	21
Oregon ash	—	—	20	20
Oregon white oak	—	121	22	143
Pacific madrone	—	—	5	5
Red alder	32	236	177	445
Total	32	398	287	717
Nonstocked[c]	—	2	12	14
Unclassified[d]	—	91	59	150
All types	411	4,382	1,400	6,194

— = less than 500,000 cubic feet found.

[a] Totals may be off because of rounding; data subject to sampling error.

[b] Includes growing-stock trees 5 inches in d.b.h. and larger.

[c] Nonstocked areas are less than 10 percent stocked with live trees.

[d] Includes volume from access-denied project areas.

Table 16d—Estimated net volume of growing-stock on nonfederal timberland, by forest type and owner class, southwest Oregon, January 1, 1997[a][b]

Forest type	Other public	Forest industry	Other private	All owners
	Million cubic feet			
Softwood:				
Douglas-fir	784	2,904	1,259	4,947
Grand fir	—	80	51	131
Incense-cedar	—	68	56	125
Ponderosa pine	—	9	43	52
Port-Orford-cedar	—	17	7	24
Redwood	—	38	—	38
Sitka spruce	—	22	34	56
Western hemlock	—	58	—	59
Western redcedar	—	50	26	75
White fir	—	56	13	69
Total	784	3,302	1,490	5,576
Hardwood:				
Apple	—	2	—	2
Bigleaf maple	—	60	1	61
California black oak	—	4	66	70
California-laurel	—	122	—	122
Canyon live oak	—	31	—	31
Oregon white oak	—	92	27	119
Pacific madrone	45	229	189	464
Red alder	70	592	157	819
Tanoak	—	190	71	261
Willow	—	—	3	3
Total	116	1,323	514	1,952
Nonstocked[c]	—	—	10	10
All types	900	4,625	2,014	7,538

— = less than 500,000 cubic feet found.

[a] Totals may be off because of rounding; data subject to sampling error.

[b] Includes growing-stock trees 5 inches in d.b.h. and larger.

[c] Nonstocked areas are less than 10 percent stocked with live trees.

Table 17a—Estimated net volume of sawtimber on nonfederal timberland, by Forest type and owner class, western Oregon, January 1, 1997[a][b]

Forest type	Other public	Forest industry	Other private	All owners
	Million board feet, Scribner rule			
Softwood:				
Douglas-fir	12,754	30,485	12,412	55,651
Grand fir	—	552	260	812
Incense-cedar	—	186	132	318
Jeffrey pine	—	—	1	1
Noble fir	18	5	—	23
Pacific silver fir	—	2	—	2
Ponderosa pine	—	42	143	186
Port-Orford-cedar	—	29	10	39
Redwood	—	148	—	148
Sitka spruce	99	1,427	598	2,125
Western hemlock	1,911	5,323	219	7,453
Western redcedar	159	419	572	1,149
White fir	—	142	50	192
Total	14,941	38,761	14,398	68,099
Hardwood:				
Apple	—	7	7	14
Bigleaf maple	281	468	745	1,494
Black cottonwood	—	75	29	104
California black oak	—	5	206	211
California-laurel	—	389	—	389
Canyon live oak	—	115	—	115
Cherry	2	—	7	9
Oregon ash	—	—	78	78
Oregon white oak	—	602	368	970
Pacific madrone	112	416	325	854
Red alder	2,162	4,110	2,795	9,068
Tanoak	—	440	206	646
Willow	—	—	6	6
Total	2,558	6,627	4,773	13,958
Nonstocked[c]	—	36	187	223
Unclassified[d]	—	1,250	322	1,572
All types	17,499	46,674	19,680	83,852

— = less than 500,000 board feet found.

[a] Totals may be off because of rounding; data subject to sampling error.

[b] Includes softwood sawtimber trees 9.0 inches in d.b.h. and larger and hardwood sawtimber trees 11.0 inches in d.b.h. and larger.

[c] Nonstocked areas are less than 10 percent stocked with live trees.

[d] Includes volume from access-denied project areas.

Table 17b—Estimated net volume of sawtimber on nonfederal timberland, by forest type and owner class, northwest Oregon, January 1, 1997[a][b]

Forest type	Other public	Forest industry	Other private	All owners
	Million board feet, Scribner rule			
Softwood:				
Douglas-fir	7,552	9,581	4,971	22,104
Grand fir	—	—	57	57
Noble fir	18	5	—	23
Pacific silver fir	—	2	—	2
Sitka spruce	99	577	82	758
Western hemlock	1,911	3,454	108	5,472
Western redcedar	159	238	492	889
Total	9,738	13,857	5,710	29,306
Hardwood:				
Apple	—	—	7	7
Bigleaf maple	281	191	633	1,105
Black cottonwood	—	75	29	104
Cherry	2	—	7	9
Oregon ash	—	—	4	4
Oregon white oak	—	5	288	294
Red alder	1,759	1,317	1,718	4,794
Total	2,043	1,588	2,687	6,318
Nonstocked[c]	—	28	113	140
Unclassified[d]	—	963	75	1,038
All types	11,781	16,436	8,585	36,802

— = less than 500,000 board feet found.

[a] Totals may be off because of rounding; data subject to sampling error.

[b] Includes softwood sawtimber trees 9.0 inches in d.b.h. and larger and hardwood sawtimber trees 11.0 inches in d.b.h. and larger.

[c] Nonstocked areas are less than 10 percent stocked with live trees.

[d] Includes volume from access-denied project areas.

Table 17c—Estimated net volume of sawtimber on nonfederal timberland, by forest type and owner class, west-central Oregon, January 1, 1997[a][b]

Forest type	Other public	Forest industry	Other private	All owners
	Million board feet, Scribner rule			
Softwood:				
Douglas-fir	1,752	11,573	3,261	16,587
Grand fir	—	170	23	193
Incense-cedar	—	38	—	38
Ponderosa pine	—	—	20	20
Sitka spruce	—	761	381	1,142
Western hemlock	—	1,684	111	1,796
Western redcedar	—	26	7	33
Total	1,752	14,252	3,804	19,809
Hardwood:				
Bigleaf maple	—	111	111	222
California black oak	—	—	36	36
Oregon ash	—	—	74	74
Oregon white oak	—	327	40	367
Pacific madrone	—	—	9	9
Red alder	97	787	637	1,521
Total	97	1,226	908	2,230
Nonstocked[c]	—	8	47	55
Unclassified[d]	—	286	247	533
All types	1,849	15,773	5,006	22,627

— = less than 500,000 board feet found.

[a] Totals may be off because of rounding; data subject to sampling error.

[b] Includes softwood sawtimber trees 9.0 inches in d.b.h. and larger and hardwood sawtimber trees 11.0 inches in d.b.h. and larger.

[c] Nonstocked areas are less than 10 percent stocked with live trees.

[d] Includes volume from access-denied project areas.

Table 17d—Estimated net volume of sawtimber on nonfederal timberland, by forest type and owner class, southwest Oregon, January 1, 1997[a][b]

Forest type	Other public	Forest industry	Other private	All owners
	Million board feet, Scribner rule			
Softwood:				
Douglas-fir	3,450	9,331	4,179	16,960
Grand fir	—	382	179	561
Incense-cedar	—	148	132	280
Jeffrey pine	—	—	1	1
Ponderosa pine	—	42	123	166
Port-Orford-cedar	—	29	10	39
Redwood	—	148	—	148
Sitka spruce	—	90	134	224
Western hemlock	—	185	—	185
Western redcedar	—	154	73	227
White fir	—	142	50	192
Total	3,450	10,651	4,883	18,985
Hardwood:				
Apple	—	7	—	7
Bigleaf maple	—	166	1	167
California black oak	—	5	170	174
California-laurel	—	389	—	389
Canyon live oak	—	115	—	115
Oregon white oak	—	270	40	309
Pacific madrone	112	416	316	844
Red alder	306	2,006	441	2,753
Tanoak	—	440	206	646
Willow	—	—	6	6
Total	419	3,813	1,178	5,411
Nonstocked[c]	—	—	28	28
All types	3,869	14,465	6,090	24,423

— = less than 500,000 board feet found.

[a] Totals may be off because of rounding; data subject to sampling error.

[b] Includes softwood sawtimber trees 9.0 inches in d.b.h. and larger and hardwood sawtimber trees 11.0 inches in d.b.h. and larger.

[c] Nonstocked areas are less than 10 percent stocked with live trees.

Table 18a—Estimated net volume of timber on nonfederal timberland, by class of timber and species group, western Oregon, January 1, 1997[a][b]

Class of timber	Softwood species	Hardwood species	All species
	Million cubic feet		
Growing-stock trees:			
Sawtimber trees			
Saw-log portion	16,958	2,366	19,323
Upper stem portion	608	638	1,246
Total, sawtimber	17,566	3,004	20,570
Poletimber trees	1,617	1,328	2,945
All growing-stock trees	19,183	4,332	23,514
Cull trees:			
Sound cull	38	161	199
Rotten cull	112	200	341
Total, cull trees	150	361	540
All timber	19,333	4,693	24,054

— = less than 500,000 cubic feet found.
[a] Totals may be off because of rounding; data subject to sampling error.
[b] Includes growing-stock trees 5 inches in d.b.h. and larger.

Table 18b—Estimated net volume of timber on nonfederal timberland, by class of timber and species group, northwest Oregon, January 1, 1997[a][b]

Class of timber	Softwood species	Hardwood species	All species
	Million cubic feet		
Growing-stock trees:			
Sawtimber trees			
Saw-log portion	7,232	1,094	8,326
Upper stem portion	246	223	469
Total, sawtimber	7,478	1,317	8,795
Poletimber trees	510	477	987
All growing-stock trees	7,988	1,794	9,782
Cull trees:			
Sound cull	7	35	42
Rotten cull	34	80	114
Total, cull trees	41	115	156
All timber	8,029	1,909	9,938

— = less than 500,000 cubic feet found.
[a] Totals may be off because of rounding; data subject to sampling error.
[b] Includes growing-stock trees 5 inches in d.b.h. and larger.

Table 18c—Estimated net volume of timber on nonfederal timberland, by class of timber and species group, west-central Oregon, January 1, 1997[a][b]

Class of timber	Softwood species	Hardwood species	All species
	Million cubic feet		
Growing-stock trees:			
Sawtimber trees			
Saw-log portion	4,694	484	5,178
Upper stem portion	166	144	310
Total, sawtimber	4,860	628	5,488
Poletimber trees	452	253	705
All growing-stock trees	5,312	881	6,193
Cull trees:			
Sound cull	2	21	23
Rotten cull	8	33	41
Total, cull trees	10	54	65
All timber	5,322	935	6,257

— = less than 500,000 cubic feet found.

[a] Totals may be off because of rounding; data subject to sampling error.

[b] Includes growing-stock trees 5 inches in d.b.h. and larger.

Table 18d—Estimated net volume of timber on nonfederal timberland, by class of timber and species group, southwest Oregon, January 1, 1997[a][b]

Class of timber	Softwood species	Hardwood species	All species
	Million cubic feet		
Growing-stock trees:			
Sawtimber trees			
Saw-log portion	5,032	788	5,820
Upper-stem portion	196	271	467
Total, sawtimber	5,228	1,059	6,287
Poletimber trees	654	598	1,252
All growing-stock trees	5,882	1,657	7,539
Cull trees:			
Sound cull	29	105	134
Rotten cull	70	87	157
Total, cull trees	99	192	291
All timber	5,981	1,849	7,830

— = less than 500,000 cubic feet found.

[a] Totals may be off because of rounding; data subject to sampling error.

[b] Includes growing-stock trees 5 inches in d.b.h. and larger.

Table 19a—Estimated current net annual growth of growing-stock on nonfederal timberland, by forest type and owner class, western Oregon, January 1, 1997[a][b]

Forest type	Other public	Forest industry	Other private	All owners
		Thousand cubic feet		
Softwood:				
Douglas-fir	101,817	385,693	98,654	586,164
Grand fir	—	4,391	3,517	7,907
Incense-cedar	—	3,744	1,753	5,497
Jeffrey pine	—	—	38	38
Noble fir	969	1,037	—	2,006
Pacific silver fir	—	180	—	180
Ponderosa pine	—	176	1,946	2,122
Port-Orford-cedar	—	1,265	221	1,486
Redwood	—	735	—	735
Sitka spruce	1,430	12,626	3,435	17,491
Western hemlock	11,360	74,958	3,651	89,969
Western redcedar	278	4,674	2,511	7,464
White fir	—	2,514	148	2,662
Total	115,854	491,993	115,875	723,722
Hardwood:				
Apple	—	174	42	215
Bigleaf maple	1,500	6,697	5,326	13,523
Black cottonwood	—	455	312	767
California black oak	—	178	1,692	1,870
California-laurel	—	3,412	—	3,412
Canyon live oak	—	486	—	486
Cherry	194	—	139	333
Oregon ash	—	—	439	439
Oregon white oak	—	3,508	4,723	8,231
Pacific madrone	783	4,518	7,304	12,605
Red alder	20,981	38,500	27,938	87,418
Tanoak	—	10,731	2,213	12,944
Willow	—	—	276	276
Total	23,458	68,658	50,403	142,518
Nonstocked[c]	—	211	1,073	1,284
Unclassified[d]	—	16,546	1,579	18,125
All types	139,312	577,408	168,930	885,649

— = less than 500 cubic feet found.

[a] Totals may be off because of rounding; data subject to sampling error.

[b] Includes growing-stock trees 5 inches in d.b.h. and larger.

[c] Nonstocked areas are less than 10 percent stocked with live trees.

[d] Includes volume from access-denied project areas.

Table 19b—Estimated current net annual growth of growing-stock on nonfederal timberland, by forest type and owner class, northwest Oregon, January 1, 1997[a][b]

Forest type	Other public	Forest industry	Other private	All owners
	Thousand cubic feet			
Softwood:				
Douglas-fir	75,937	97,112	33,588	206,638
Grand fir	—	—	966	966
Noble fir	969	912	—	1,881
Pacific silver fir	—	180	—	180
Sitka spruce	1,430	8,080	325	9,835
Western hemlock	11,360	54,515	2,672	68,548
Western redcedar	278	3,563	1,507	5,348
Total	89,974	164,363	39,057	293,394
Hardwood:				
Apple	—	—	42	42
Bigleaf maple	1,500	1,424	3,226	6,150
Black cottonwood	—	455	312	767
Cherry	194	—	139	333
Oregon ash	—	—	70	70
Oregon white oak	—	30	3,287	3,316
Red alder	18,454	8,986	13,751	41,191
Total	20,147	10,894	20,827	51,869
Nonstocked[c]	—	204	641	845
Unclassified[d]	—	13,232	298	13,530
All types	110,122	188,692	60,824	359,638

— = less than 500 cubic feet found.

[a] Totals may be off because of rounding; data subject to sampling error.

[b] Includes growing-stock trees 5 inches in d.b.h. and larger.

[c] Nonstocked areas are less than 10 percent stocked with live trees.

[d] Includes volume from access-denied project areas.

Table 19c—Estimated current net annual growth of growing-stock on non-federal timberland, by forest type and owner class, west-central Oregon, January 1, 1997[a][b]

Forest type	Other public	Forest industry	Other private	All owners
		Thousand cubic feet		
Softwood:				
Douglas-fir	8,761	146,170	26,665	181,596
Grand fir	—	2,595	909	3,504
Incense-cedar	—	387	—	387
Noble fir	—	125	—	125
Ponderosa pine	—	—	424	424
Sitka spruce	—	3,995	2,227	6,221
Western hemlock	—	18,034	640	18,674
Western redcedar	—	168	155	322
Total	8,761	171,473	31,020	211,254
Hardwood:				
Bigleaf maple	—	2,775	2,073	4,848
California black oak	—	—	184	184
Oregon ash	—	—	369	369
Oregon white oak	—	2,422	1,095	3,516
Pacific madrone	—	—	386	386
Red alder	1,095	8,971	5,395	15,461
Total	1,095	14,167	9,502	24,764
Nonstocked[c]	—	7	333	340
Unclassified[d]	—	3,314	1,280	4,595
All types	9,856	188,962	42,135	240,953

— = less than 500 cubic feet found.

[a] Totals may be off because of rounding; data subject to sampling error.

[b] Includes growing-stock trees 5 inches in d.b.h. and larger.

[c] Nonstocked areas are less than 10 percent stocked with live trees.

[d] Includes volume from access-denied project areas.

Table 19d—Estimated current net annual growth of growing-stock on nonfederal timberland, by forest type and owner class, southwest Oregon, January 1, 1997[a][b]

Forest type	Other public	Forest industry	Other private	All owners
		Thousand cubic feet		
Softwood:				
Douglas-fir	17,119	142,411	38,401	197,930
Grand fir	—	1,796	1,642	3,438
Incense-cedar	—	3,357	1,753	5,110
Jeffrey pine	—	—	38	38
Ponderosa pine	—	176	1,522	1,698
Port-Orford-cedar	—	1,265	221	1,486
Redwood	—	735	—	735
Sitka spruce	—	551	884	1,435
Western hemlock	—	2,409	339	2,748
Western redcedar	—	944	850	1,794
White fir	—	2,514	148	2,662
Total	17,119	156,157	45,798	219,074
Hardwood:				
Apple	—	174	—	174
Bigleaf maple	—	2,498	27	2,525
California black oak	—	178	1,508	1,685
California-laurel	—	3,412	—	3,412
Canyon live oak	—	486	—	486
Oregon white oak	—	1,057	341	1,398
Pacific madrone	783	4,518	6,918	12,219
Red alder	1,432	20,543	8,791	30,766
Tanoak	—	10,731	2,213	12,944
Willow	—	—	276	276
Total	2,215	43,596	20,074	65,885
Nonstocked[c]	—	—	98	98
All types	19,334	199,753	65,971	285,058

— = less than 500 cubic feet found.
[a] Totals may be off because of rounding; data subject to sampling error.
[b] Includes growing-stock trees 5 inches in d.b.h. and larger.
[c] Nonstocked areas are less than 10 percent stocked with live trees.

Table 20a—Estimated gross annual growth of growing-stock on nonfederal timberland, by owner class and species group, western Oregon, January 1, 1997[a]

Class of timber and owner class	Average volume	Species group		All species
		Softwoods	Hardwoods	
	Cubic feet per acre	– – – – – *Thousand cubic feet* – – – – –		
Growing-stock:[b]				
Other public	188	131,346	28,910	160,256
Forest industry	153	561,140	79,860	641,001
Other private	105	146,623	51,365	197,988
Total, growing-stock	145	839,110	160,135	999,245

[a] Totals may be off because of rounding; data subject to sampling error.
[b] Includes growing-stock trees 5.0 inches in d.b.h. and larger.

Table 20b—Estimated gross annual growth of growing-stock on nonfederal timberland, by owner class and species group, northwest Oregon, January 1, 1997[a]

Class of timber and owner class	Average volume	Species group		All species
		Softwoods	Hardwoods	
	Cubic feet per acre	– – – – – *Thousand cubic feet* – – – – –		
Growing-stock:[b]				
Other public	218	101,344	24,132	125,476
Forest industry	192	189.024	23,597	212,621
Other private	104	49,470	22,732	72,202
Total, growing-stock	173	339,839	70,461	410,299

[a] Totals may be off because of rounding; data subject to sampling error.
[b] Includes growing-stock trees 5.0 inches in d.b.h. and larger.

Table 20c—Estimated gross annual growth of growing-stock on nonfederal timberland, by owner class and species group, west-central Oregon, January 1, 1997[a]

Class of timber and owner class	Average volume	Species group Softwoods	Species group Hardwoods	All species
	Cubic feet per acre	— — — — *Thousand cubic feet*— — — —		
Growing-stock:[b]				
Other public	122	10,015	1,839	11,854
Forest industry	155	188,053	19,055	207,108
Other private	116	37,674	12,095	49,769
Total, growing-stock	144	235,742	32,989	268,731

[a] Totals may be off because of rounding; data subject to sampling error.
[b] Includes growing-stock trees 5.0 inches in d.b.h. and larger.

Table 20d—Estimated gross annual growth of growing-stock on non-federal timberland, by owner class and species group, southwest Oregon, January 1, 1997[a]

Class of timber and owner class	Average volume	Species group Softwoods	Species group Hardwoods	All species
	Cubic feet per acre	— — — — *Thousand cubic feet* — — — —		
Growing-stock:[b]				
Other public	128	19,987	2,939	22,926
Forest industry	127	184,063	37,208	221,272
Other private	100	59,479	16,538	76,017
Total, growing-stock	114	263,529	56,685	320,214

[a] Totals may be off because of rounding; data subject to sampling error.
[b] Includes growing-stock trees 5.0 inches in d.b.h. and larger.

Table 21a—Estimated current net annual growth of sawtimber on nonfederal timberland, by forest type and owner class, western Oregon, January 1, 1997[a][b]

Forest type	Other public	Forest industry	Other private	All owners
	Thousand board feet, Scribner rule			
Softwood:				
Douglas-fir	474,257	1,568,053	432,070	2,474,381
Grand fir	—	16,891	10,377	27,268
Incense-cedar	—	13,253	5,602	18,856
Jeffrey pine	—	—	188	188
Noble fir	2,646	1,715	—	4,361
Pacific silver fir	—	293	—	293
Ponderosa pine	—	1,026	5,740	6,766
Port-Orford-cedar	—	3,290	466	3,756
Redwood	—	3,885	—	3,885
Sitka spruce	7,096	57,453	16,111	80,660
Western hemlock	54,624	316,172	6,659	377,455
Western redcedar	1,614	11,847	10,621	24,081
White fir	—	4,929	688	5,617
Total	540,237	1,998,808	488,525	3,027,569
Hardwood:				
Apple	—	1,167	113	1,280
Bigleaf maple	7,177	21,005	20,677	48,859
Black cottonwood	—	2,455	511	2,966
California black oak	—	100	5,075	5,174
California-laurel	—	10,418	—	10,418
Canyon live oak	—	1,418	—	1,418
Cherry	381	—	218	599
Oregon ash	—	—	1,555	1,555
Oregon white oak	—	12,929	13,605	26,534
Pacific madrone	2,458	23,041	22,110	47,610
Red alder	87,420	170,778	112,236	370,434
Tanoak	—	29,566	6,285	35,850
Willow	—	—	767	767
Total	97,437	272,877	183,152	553,466
Nonstocked[c]	—	1,067	3,967	5,034
Unclassified[d]	—	87,443	7,930	95,373
All types	637,673	2,360,195	683,574	3,681,442

— = less than 500 board feet found.

[a] Totals may be off because of rounding; data subject to sampling error.

[b] Includes softwood sawtimber trees 9.0 inches in d.b.h. and larger and hardwood sawtimber trees 11.0 inches in d.b.h. and larger.

[c] Nonstocked areas are less than 10 percent stocked with live trees.

[d] Includes volume from access-denied project areas.

Table 21b—Estimated current net annual growth of sawtimber on nonfederal timberland, by forest type and owner class, northwest Oregon, January 1, 1997[a][b]

Forest type	Other public	Forest industry	Other private	All owners
	Thousand board feet, Scribner rule			
Softwood:				
Douglas-fir	358,282	414,181	172,494	944,958
Grand fir	—	—	3,159	3,159
Noble fir	2,646	1,715	—	4,361
Pacific silver fir	—	293	—	293
Sitka spruce	7,096	34,332	1,375	42,803
Western hemlock	54,624	228,152	3,848	286,623
Western redcedar	1,614	6,683	7,556	15,853
Total	424,261	685,357	188,432	1,298,050
Hardwood:				
Apple	—	—	113	113
Bigleaf maple	7,177	5,935	14,579	27,691
Black cottonwood	—	2,455	511	2,966
Cherry	381	—	218	599
Oregon ash	—	—	120	120
Oregon white oak	—	79	10,184	10,263
Red alder	78,785	37,011	63,750	179,546
Total	86,344	45,480	89,476	221,300
Nonstocked[c]	—	1,032	2,343	3,375
Unclassified[d]	—	74,193	3,986	78,179
All types	510,605	805,030	281,893	1,597,529

— = less than 500 board feet found.

[a] Totals may be off because of rounding; data subject to sampling error.

[b] Includes softwood sawtimber trees 9.0 inches in d.b.h. and larger and hardwood sawtimber trees 11.0 inches in d.b.h. and larger.

[c] Nonstocked areas are less than 10 percent stocked with live trees.

[d] Includes volume from access-denied project areas.

Table 21c—Estimated current net annual growth of sawtimber on nonfederal timberland, by forest type and owner class, west-central Oregon, January 1, 1997[a][b]

Forest type	Other public	Forest industry	Other private	All owners
	Thousand board feet, Scribner rule			
Softwood:				
Douglas-fir	44,080	623,097	117,318	784,495
Grand fir	—	8,298	1,757	10,056
Incense-cedar	—	1,229	—	1,229
Ponderosa pine	—	—	2,083	2,083
Sitka spruce	—	20,614	10,389	31,003
Western hemlock	—	80,578	2,812	83,389
Western redcedar	—	854	698	1,552
Total	44,080	734,670	135,058	913,808
Hardwood:				
Bigleaf maple	—	7,340	6,072	13,413
California black oak	—	—	297	297
Oregon ash	—	—	1,435	1,435
Oregon white oak	—	8,824	2,593	11,417
Pacific madrone	—	—	2,896	2,896
Red alder	5,143	38,705	20,352	64,200
Total	5,143	54,869	33,645	93,657
Nonstocked[c]	—	35	1,257	1,292
Unclassified[d]	—	14,316	7,545	21,861
All types	49,222	803,855	176,248	1,029,326

— = less than 500 board feet found.

[a] Totals may be off because of rounding; data subject to sampling error.

[b] Includes softwood sawtimber trees 9.0 inches in d.b.h. and larger and hardwood sawtimber trees 11.0 inches in d.b.h. and larger.

[c] Nonstocked areas are less than 10 percent stocked with live trees.

[d] Includes volume from access-denied project areas.

Table 21d—Estimated current net annual growth of sawtimber on nonfederal timberland, by forest type and owner class, southwest Oregon, January 1, 1997[a][b]

Forest type	Other public	Forest industry	Other private	All owners
	Thousand board feet, Scribner rule			
Softwood:				
Douglas-fir	71,895	530,775	142,258	744,928
Grand fir	—	8,593	5,461	14,054
Incense-cedar	—	12,024	5,602	17,626
Jeffrey pine	—	—	188	188
Ponderosa pine	—	1,026	3,657	4,683
Port-Orford-cedar	—	3,290	466	3,756
Redwood	—	3,885	—	3,885
Sitka spruce	—	2,507	4,347	6,854
Western hemlock	—	7,443	—	7,443
Western redcedar	—	4,309	2,367	6,676
White fir	—	4,929	688	5,617
Total	71,895	578,781	165,035	815,711
Hardwood:				
Apple	—	1,167	—	1,167
Bigleaf maple	—	7,730	25	7,755
California black oak	—	100	4,778	4,878
California-laurel	—	10,418	—	10,418
Canyon live oak	—	1,418	—	1,418
Oregon white oak	—	4,026	829	4,855
Pacific madrone	2,458	23,041	19,214	44,714
Red alder	3,492	95,062	28,133	126,688
Tanoak	—	29,566	6,285	35,850
Willow	—	—	767	767
Total	5,950	172,528	60,031	238,509
Nonstocked[c]	—	—	367	367
All types	77,846	751,309	225,433	1,054,588

— = less than 500 board feet found.
[a] Totals may be off because of rounding; data subject to sampling error.
[b] Includes softwood sawtimber trees 9.0 inches in d.b.h. and larger and hardwood sawtimber trees 11.0 inches in d.b.h. and larger.
[c] Nonstocked areas are less than 10 percent stocked with live trees.

Table 22a—Estimated average annual mortality of growing-stock on nonfederal timberland, by forest type and owner class, western Oregon, January 1, 1997[a][b]

Forest type	Other public	Forest industry	Other private	All owners
	Thousand cubic feet			
Softwood:				
Douglas-fir	13,575	35,065	15,782	64,422
Grand fir	—	1,182	502	1,684
Incense-cedar	—	471	528	999
Jeffrey pine	—	—	1	1
Noble fir	15	10	—	25
Pacific silver fir	—	5	—	5
Ponderosa pine	—	106	272	378
Port-Orford-cedar	—	105	196	301
Redwood	—	302	—	302
Sitka spruce	103	2,413	1,230	3,747
Western hemlock	1,709	9,747	240	11,695
Western redcedar	152	737	914	1,803
White fir	—	374	53	427
Total	15,555	50,516	19,717	85,788
Hardwood:				
Apple	—	4	9	13
Bigleaf maple	458	747	1,766	2,971
Black cottonwood	—	64	40	104
California black oak	—	12	609	621
California-laurel	—	561	—	561
Canyon live oak	—	85	—	85
Cherry	8	—	9	17
Oregon ash	—	1	127	128
Oregon white oak	—	1,403	897	2,300
Pacific madrone	344	2,047	1,337	3,729
Red alder	5,750	10,367	6,449	22,566
Tanoak	—	987	396	1,383
Willow	—	—	4	4
Total	6,560	16,279	11,643	34,482
Nonstocked[c]	—	1,697	457	2,154
All types	22,115	68,492	31,817	122,424

— = less than 500 cubic feet found.

[a] Totals may be off because of rounding; data subject to sampling error.

[b] Includes growing-stock trees 5 inches in d.b.h. and larger.

[c] Nonstocked areas are less than 10 percent stocked with live trees.

Table 22b—Estimated average annual mortality of growing-stock on nonfederal timberland, by forest type and owner class, northwest Oregon, January 1, 1997[a][b]

Forest type	Other public	Forest industry	Other private	All owners
	Thousand cubic feet			
Softwood:				
Douglas-fir	8,708	11,516	5,052	25,276
Grand fir	—	—	87	87
Noble fir	15	10	—	25
Pacific silver fir	—	5	—	5
Sitka spruce	103	1,282	57	1,442
Western hemlock	1,709	7,137	117	8,962
Western redcedar	152	463	724	1,338
Total	10,688	20,411	6,036	37,135
Hardwood:				
Apple	—	—	9	9
Bigleaf maple	458	366	1,545	2,369
Black cottonwood	—	64	40	104
Cherry	8	—	9	17
Oregon ash	—	—	12	12
Oregon white oak	—	8	581	589
Red alder	4,965	3,458	3,634	12,057
Total	5,431	3,896	5,830	15,158
Nonstocked[c]	—	70	141	211
All types	16,119	24,377	12,007	52,504

— = less than 500 cubic feet found.

[a] Totals may be off because of rounding; data subject to sampling error.

[b] Includes growing-stock trees 5 inches in d.b.h. and larger.

[c] Nonstocked areas are less than 10 percent stocked with live trees.

Table 22c—Estimated average annual mortality of growing-stock on nonfederal timberland, by forest type and owner class, west-central Oregon, January 1, 1997[a][b]

Forest type	Other public	Forest industry	Other private	All owners
	Thousand cubic feet			
Softwood:				
Douglas-fir	1,831	12,030	4,221	18,083
Grand fir	—	368	67	435
Incense-cedar	—	52	—	52
Ponderosa pine	—	—	32	32
Sitka spruce	—	972	956	1,928
Western hemlock	—	2,283	120	2,403
Western redcedar	—	17	13	30
Total	1,831	15,722	5,409	22,963
Hardwood:				
Bigleaf maple	—	125	220	344
California black oak	—	—	188	188
Oregon ash	—	—	115	115
Oregon white oak	—	582	105	687
Pacific madrone	—	—	9	9
Red alder	198	2,023	1,728	3,949
Total	198	2,730	2,365	5,293
Nonstocked[c]	—	4	83	87
All types	2,029	18,456	7,857	28,343

— = less than 500 cubic feet found.

[a] Totals may be off because of rounding; data subject to sampling error.

[b] Includes growing-stock trees 5 inches in d.b.h. and larger.

Table 22d—Estimated average annual mortality of growing stock on nonfederal timberland, by forest type and owner class, southwest Oregon, January 1, 1997[a][b]

Forest type	Other public	Forest industry	Other private	All owners
	Thousand cubic feet			
Softwood types:				
Douglas-fir	2,701	10,107	4,681	17,489
Grand fir	—	793	323	1,116
Incense-cedar	—	184	310	494
Jeffrey pine	—	—	—	—
Ponderosa pine	—	36	175	211
Port-Orford-cedar	—	35	57	92
Redwood	—	102	—	102
Sitka spruce	—	79	140	219
Western hemlock	—	304	1	305
Western redcedar	—	257	168	425
White fir	—	253	13	265
Total	2,701	12,150	5,867	20,718
Hardwood types:				
Apple	—	2	—	2
Bigleaf maple	—	246	1	247
California black oak	—	7	351	358
California-laurel	—	535	—	535
Canyon live oak	—	74	—	74
Oregon white oak	—	678	197	876
Pacific madrone	234	1,496	1,156	2,885
Red alder	349	4,155	882	5,386
Tanoak	—	842	287	1,129
Willow	—	—	4	4
Total	582	8,035	2,878	11,495
Nonstocked[c]	—	—	63	63
All types	3,283	20,185	8,808	32,276

— = less than 500 cubic feet or none found.

[a] Totals may be off because of rounding; data subject to sampling error.

[b] Includes growing-stock trees 5 inches in d.b.h. and larger.

[c] Nonstocked areas are less than 10 percent stocked with live trees.

Table 23a—Estimated average annual mortality of sawtimber on nonfederal timberland, by forest type and owner class, western Oregon, January 1, 1997[a][b]

Forest type	Other public	Forest industry	Other private	All owners
	Thousand board feet, Scribner rule			
Softwood:				
Douglas-fir	47,201	109,426	50,314	206,941
Grand fir	—	4,438	1,229	5,667
Incense-cedar	—	596	802	1,398
Jeffrey pine	—	—	3	3
Noble fir	27	—	—	27
Pacific silver fir	—	3	—	3
Ponderosa pine	—	433	741	1,174
Port-Orford-cedar	—	50	44	93
Redwood	—	1,211	—	1,211
Sitka spruce	278	8,508	3,805	12,591
Western hemlock	6,217	28,733	691	35,642
Western redcedar	695	1,673	3,559	5,927
White fir	—	631	189	820
Total	54,419	155,702	61,375	271,496
Hardwood:				
Apple	—	12	23	35
Bigleaf maple	1,726	2,065	6,656	10,447
Black cottonwood	—	299	184	483
California black oak	—	14	1,267	1,281
California-laurel	—	1,688	—	1,688
Canyon live oak	—	284	—	284
Cherry	6	—	16	22
Oregon ash	—	—	469	469
Oregon white oak	—	3,608	1,585	5,193
Pacific madrone	737	2,397	1,226	4,359
Red alder	18,229	29,851	21,961	70,041
Tanoak	—	2,229	958	3,187
Willow	—	—	9	9
Total	20,697	42,447	34,355	97,499
Nonstocked[c]	—	287	953	1,240
All types	75,116	198,436	41,445	370,235

— = less than 500 board feet found.
[a] Totals may be off because of rounding; data subject to sampling error.
[b] Includes softwood sawtimber trees 9.0 inches in d.b.h. and larger and hardwood sawtimber trees 11.0 inches in d.b.h. and larger.
[c] Nonstocked areas are less than 10 percent stocked with live trees.

Table 23b—Estimated average annual mortality of sawtimber on nonfederal timberland, by forest type and owner class, northwest Oregon, January 1, 1997[a][b]

Forest type	Other public	Forest industry	Other private	All owners
	Thousand board feet, Scribner rule			
Softwood:				
Douglas-fir	27,549	39,898	19,713	87,160
Grand fir	—	—	154	154
Noble fir	27	—	—	27
Pacific silver fir	—	3	—	3
Sitka spruce	278	3,684	264	4,226
Western hemlock	6,217	20,262	304	26,783
Western redcedar	695	828	3,070	4,593
Total, softwood types	34,767	64,675	23,504	122,947
Hardwood:				
Apple	—	—	23	23
Bigleaf maple	1,726	1,284	5,960	8,969
Black cottonwood	—	299	184	483
Cherry	6	—	16	22
Oregon ash	—	—	20	20
Oregon white oak	—	18	1,129	1,148
Red alder	14,957	10,661	13,351	38,969
Total, hardwood types	16,689	12,263	20,684	49,635
Nonstocked[c]	—	266	424	690
All types	51,456	77,204	44,612	173,272

— = less than 500 board feet found.

[a] Totals may be off because of rounding; data subject to sampling error.

[b] Includes softwood sawtimber trees 9.0 inches in d.b.h. and larger and hardwood sawtimber trees 11.0 inches in d.b.h. and larger.

[c] Nonstocked areas are less than 10 percent stocked with live trees.

Table 23c—Estimated average annual mortality of sawtimber on nonfederal timberland, by forest type and owner class, west-central Oregon, January 1, 1997[a][b]

Forest type	Other public	Forest industry	Other private	All owners
	Thousand board feet, Scribner rule			
Softwood:				
Douglas-fir	7,632	37,473	13,266	58,370
Grand fir	—	678	56	734
Incense-cedar	—	101	—	101
Ponderosa pine	—	—	103	103
Sitka spruce	—	4,300	3,029	7,329
Western hemlock	—	7,880	387	8,267
Western redcedar	—	78	37	116
Total, softwood types	7,632	50,510	16,879	75,020
Hardwood:				
Bigleaf maple	—	305	696	1,001
California black oak	—	—	406	406
Oregon ash	—	—	449	449
Oregon white oak	—	1,543	173	1,715
Pacific madrone	—	—	16	16
Red alder	539	5,988	5,758	12,285
Total, hardwood types	539	7,835	7,498	15,872
Nonstocked[c]	—	21	311	332
All types	8,171	58,366	24,688	91,224

— = less than 500 board feet found.

[a] Totals may be off because of rounding; data subject to sampling error.

[b] Includes softwood sawtimber trees 9.0 inches in d.b.h. and larger and hardwood sawtimber trees 11.0 inches in d.b.h. and larger.

[c] Nonstocked areas are less than 10 percent stocked with live trees.

Table 23d—Estimated average annual mortality of sawtimber on nonfederal timberland, by forest type and owner class, southwest Oregon, January 1, 1997[a b]

Forest type	Other public	Forest industry	Other private	All owners
	Thousand board feet, Scribner rule			
Softwood:				
Douglas-fir	12,020	32,055	17,336	61,410
Grand fir	—	3,760	1,019	4,779
Incense-cedar	—	495	802	1,296
Jeffrey pine	—	—	3	3
Ponderosa pine	—	433	637	1,070
Port-Orford-cedar	—	50	44	93
Redwood	—	1,211	—	1,211
Sitka spruce	—	523	512	1,035
Western hemlock	—	592	—	592
Western redcedar	—	767	452	1,219
White fir	—	631	189	820
Total, softwood types	12,020	40,517	20,992	73,529
Hardwood:				
Apple	—	12	—	12
Bigleaf maple	—	476	1	477
California black oak	—	14	860	874
California-laurel	—	1,688	—	1,688
Canyon live oak	—	284	—	284
Oregon white oak	—	2,047	283	2,330
Pacific madrone	737	2,397	1,210	4,343
Red alder	2,733	13,202	2,853	18,787
Tanoak	—	2,229	958	3,187
Willow	—	—	9	9
Total, hardwood types	3,469	22,349	6,173	31,992
Nonstocked[c]	—	—	288	288
All types	15,489	62,866	27,453	105,809

— = less than 500 board feet found.

[a] Totals may be off because of rounding; data subject to sampling error.

[b] Includes softwood sawtimber trees 9.0 inches in d.b.h. and larger and hardwood sawtimber trees 11.0 inches in d.b.h. and larger.

[c] Nonstocked areas are less than 10 percent stocked with live trees.

Table 24a—Estimated area, net volume of growing-stock, and net volume of sawtimber on nonfederal timberland, by stand age and owner class, western Oregon, January 1, 1997[a,b,c]

Stand age	Other public			Forest industry			Other private			All owners		
	Area	Growing-stock volume	Sawtimber volume	Area	Growing-stock volume	Sawtimber volume	Area	Growing-stock volume	Sawtimber volume	Area	Growing-stock volume	Sawtimber volume
	Thousand acres	Million cubic feet	Million board feet[d]	Thousand acres	Million cubic feet	Million board feet[d]	Thousand acres	Million cubic feet	Million board feet[d]	Thousand acres	Million cubic feet	Million board feet[d]
Even aged:												
0-9	39	22	103	513	79	229	171	19	74	723	120	405
10-19	56	21	64	612	170	293	217	239	676	886	430	1,034
20-29	117	165	352	879	1,405	2,803	232	304	703	1,229	1,874	3,858
30-39	158	660	2,058	637	2,647	7,595	170	490	1,468	965	3,796	11,121
40-49	183	1,100	3,940	552	2,931	10,690	297	1,143	3,836	1,031	5,173	18,466
50-59	66	573	2,570	332	2,515	10,195	187	936	3,497	584	4,025	16,262
60-69	63	575	2,570	136	1,038	4,375	97	467	1,787	296	2,080	8,732
70-79	10	141	662	37	281	1,331	75	439	1,854	122	861	3,848
80-89	—	—	—	21	89	201	16	98	387	36	187	588
90-99	24	198	979	17	87	336	10	31	96	51	316	1,412
100-109	26	241	1,247	11	94	449	15	27	81	52	362	1,777
110-119	—	—	—	18	115	348	17	70	285	36	185	633
120-129	9	108	575	—	—	—	3	—	—	12	108	575
130-139	—	—	—	—	—	—	—	—	—	—	—	—
140-149	—	—	—	—	—	—	—	—	—	—	—	—
150-159	5	38	191	—	—	—	2	69	392	7	106	583
160-169	—	—	—	—	—	—	—	—	—	—	—	—
170-179	—	—	—	—	—	—	—	—	—	—	—	—
180-189	—	—	—	—	—	—	—	—	—	—	—	—
190-199	—	—	—	—	—	—	—	—	—	—	—	—
200-299	—	—	—	—	—	—	—	—	—	—	—	—
300+	—	—	—	—	—	—	—	—	—	—	—	—
Uneven aged:												
<100	68	467	1,936	237	1,094	3,979	240	948	3,383	545	2,509	9,297
100+	21	77	251	82	591	2,564	45	182	622	148	850	3,436
Nonstocked[e]	6	—	—	37	8	36	68	69	218	111	77	254
Unclassified[f]	—	—	—	56	376	1,250	20	77	322	75	453	1,572
Total, all ages	850	4,386	17,449	4,177	13,521	46,674	1,882	5,608	19,680	6,910	23,515	83,852

— = less than 500 acres, 500,000 cubic feet, or 500,000 board feet.

[a] Totals may be off because of rounding; data subject to sampling error.

[b] Includes growing-stock trees 5.0 inches in d.b.h. and larger.

[c] Includes softwood sawtimber trees 9.0 inches in d.b.h. and larger, and hardwood sawtimber trees 11.0 inches in d.b.h. and larger.

[d] Scr bner rule.

[e] Nonstocked areas are less than 10 percent stocked with live trees.

[f] Includes volume from access-denied project areas.

Table 24b—Estimated area, net volume of growing-stock, and net volume of sawtimber on nonfederal timberland, by stand age and owner class, northwest Oregon, January 1, 1997[a,b,c]

Stand age	Other public			Forest industry			Other private			All owners		
	Area	Growing-stock volume	Sawtimber volume[d]	Area	Growing-stock volume	Sawtimber volume[d]	Area	Growing-stock volume	Sawtimber volume[d]	Area	Growing-stock volume	Sawtimber volume[d]
	Thousand acres	Million cubic feet	Million board feet	Thousand acres	Million cubic feet	Million board feet	Thousand acres	Million cubic feet	Million board feet	Thousand acres	Million cubic feet	Million board feet
Even aged:												
0-09	8	8	39	137	13	49	74	11	50	220	32	137
10-19	42	15	39	109	32	57	77	114	417	228	160	513
20-29	64	130	297	241	400	819	93	104	263	399	634	1,379
30-39	137	566	1,766	182	859	2,578	66	210	658	385	1,635	5,002
40-49	161	1,003	3,578	147	845	3,116	127	457	1,725	435	2,306	8,419
50-59	54	438	1,910	137	1,248	5,130	47	259	1,090	238	1,944	8,130
60-69	38	362	1,668	59	571	2,522	49	240	965	145	1,173	5,155
70-79	10	141	662	20	219	1,046	49	344	1,557	79	704	3,265
80-89	—	—	—	1	4	19	7	47	215	7	47	215
90-99	7	38	188	—	—	—	1	9	37	10	51	243
100-109	8	73	418	—	—	—	—	—	—	8	73	418
110-119	—	—	—	—	—	—	4	18	86	4	18	86
120-129	—	—	—	—	—	—	—	—	—	—	—	—
130-139	—	—	—	—	—	—	—	—	—	—	—	—
140-149	—	—	—	—	—	—	—	—	—	—	—	—
150-159	—	—	—	—	—	—	—	—	—	—	—	—
160-169	—	—	—	—	—	—	—	—	—	—	—	—
170-179	—	—	—	—	—	—	—	—	—	—	—	—
180-189	—	—	—	—	—	—	—	—	—	—	—	—
190-199	—	—	—	—	—	—	—	—	—	—	—	—
200-299	—	—	—	—	—	—	—	—	—	—	—	—
300+	—	—	—	—	—	—	—	—	—	—	—	—
Uneven aged:												
<100	40	302	1,215	9	31	111	69	300	1,215	118	632	2,541
>100	—	—	—	—	—	—	5	26	120	5	26	120
Nonstocked[e]	5	—	—	15	7	28	22	38	113	42	45	140
Unclassified[f]	—	—	—	44	285	963	3	18	75	47	303	1,038
Total, all ages	574	3,075	11,781	1,101	4,514	16,437	693	2,194	8,585	2,370	9,783	36,802

— = less than 500 acres, 500,000 cubic feet, or 500,000 board feet.
[a] Totals may be off because of rounding; data subject to sampling error.
[b] Includes growing-stock trees 5.0 inches in d.b.h. and larger.
[c] Includes softwood sawtimber trees 9.0 inches in d.b.h. and larger, and hardwood sawtimber trees 11.0 inches in d.b.h. and larger.
[d] Scribner rule.
[e] Nonstocked areas are less than 10 percent stocked with live trees.
[f] Includes volume from access-denied project areas

Table 24c—Estimated area, net volume of growing-stock, and net volume of sawtimber on nonfederal timberland, by stand age and owner class, west-central Oregon, January 1, 1997[a][b][c]

Stand age	Other public			Forest industry			Other private			All owners		
	Area	Growing-stock volume	Sawtimber volume[d]	Area	Growing-stock volume	Sawtimber volume[d]	Area	Growing-stock volume	Sawtimber volume[d]	Area	Growing-stock volume	Sawtimber volume[d]
	Thousand acres	Million cubic feet	Million board feet	Thousand acres	Million cubic feet	Million board feet	Thousand acres	Million cubic feet	Million board feet	Thousand acres	Million cubic feet	Million board feet
Even aged:												
0-09	8	—	—	171	9	45	52	6	19	231	15	64
10-19	14	7	25	213	54	98	37	42	102	264	103	225
20-29	26	11	13	259	444	846	43	55	116	328	510	975
30-39	—	—	—	218	791	2,321	48	121	399	266	913	2,720
40-49	9	32	97	218	1,302	4,954	45	276	949	272	1,609	5,999
50-59	12	135	660	95	620	2,600	57	370	1,440	164	1,126	4,700
60-69	15	126	574	28	166	651	7	47	160	50	339	1,385
70-79	—	—	—	9	53	268	4	11	39	13	65	307
80-89	—	—	—	4	4	8	—	—	—	4	4	8
90-99	—	—	—	7	25	98	1	5	7	9	29	105
100-109	9	63	288	6	79	404	8	33	140	15	142	692
110-119	—	—	—	4	29	79	—	—	—	12	62	218
120-129	—	—	—	—	—	—	—	—	—	—	—	—
130-139	—	—	—	—	—	—	—	—	—	—	—	—
140-149	—	—	—	—	—	—	—	—	—	—	—	—
150-159	5	38	191	—	—	—	—	—	—	5	38	191
160-169	—	—	—	—	—	—	—	—	—	—	—	—
170-179	—	—	—	—	—	—	—	—	—	—	—	—
180-189	—	—	—	—	—	—	—	—	—	—	—	—
190-199	—	—	—	—	—	—	—	—	—	—	—	—
200-299	—	—	—	—	—	—	—	—	—	—	—	—
300+	—	—	—	—	—	—	—	—	—	—	—	—
Uneven aged:												
<100	—	—	—	63	529	2,288	65	268	1,028	128	797	3,316
100+	—	—	—	18	184	819	18	94	313	36	278	1,133
Nonstocked[e]	—	—	—	14	2	8	29	12	47	43	14	55
Unclassified[f]	—	—	—	12	91	286	16	59	247	28	150	533
Total, all ages	98	411	1,849	1,339	4,382	15,773	431	1,400	5,006	1,867	6,194	22,627

— = less than 500 acres, 500,000 cubic feet, or 500,000 board feet.

[a] Totals may be off because of rounding; data subject to sampling error.

[b] Includes growing-stock trees 5.0 inches in d.b.h. and the larger.

[c] Includes softwood sawtimber trees 9.0 inches in d.b.h. and larger, and hardwood sawtimber trees 11.0 inches in d.b.h and larger.

[d] Scr bner rule.

[e] Nonstocked areas are less than 10 percent stocked with live trees.

[f] Includes volume from access-denied project area.

Table 24d—Estimated area, net volume of growing-stock, and net volume of sawtimber on nonfederal timberland, by stand age and owner class, southwest Oregon, January 1, 1997[a,b,c]

Stand age	Other public			Forest industry			Other private			All owners		
	Area	Growing-stock volume	Sawtimber volume	Area	Growing-stock volume	Sawtimber volume	Area	Growing-stock volume	Sawtimber volume	Area	Growing-stock volume	Sawtimber volume
	Thousand acres	Million cubic feet	Million board feet[d]	Thousand acres	Million cubic feet	Million board feet[d]	Thousand acres	Million cubic feet	Million board feet[d]	Thousand acres	Million cubic feet	Million board feet[d]
Even aged:												
0-09	23	14	64	204	56	136	45	3	4	272	73	204
19-Oct	1	—	—	291	84	138	103	83	158	395	166	295
20-29	27	25	41	379	561	1,139	95	145	323	501	730	1,503
30-39	21	93	291	237	997	2,696	56	159	411	314	1,249	3,398
40-49	13	65	265	187	784	2,620	124	410	1,163	324	1,258	4,048
50-59	—	—	—	99	648	2,465	83	307	966	182	955	3,432
60-69	10	87	327	50	301	1,203	42	180	661	101	568	2,191
70-79	—	—	—	8	8	18	22	84	259	30	93	276
80-89	—	—	—	17	85	192	9	51	173	26	137	365
90-99	17	160	792	8	59	220	8	18	53	32	237	1,064
100-109	9	106	541	5	15	45	15	27	81	29	147	667
110-119	—	—	—	14	86	269	6	19	60	20	104	329
120-129	9	108	575	—	—	—	3	—	—	12	108	575
130-139	—	—	—	—	—	—	—	—	—	—	—	—
140-149	—	—	—	—	—	—	—	—	—	—	—	—
150-159	—	—	—	—	—	—	2	69	392	2	69	392
160-169	—	—	—	—	—	—	—	—	—	—	—	—
170-179	—	—	—	—	—	—	—	—	—	—	—	—
180-189	—	—	—	—	—	—	—	—	—	—	—	—
190-199	—	—	—	—	—	—	—	—	—	—	—	—
200-299	—	—	—	—	—	—	—	—	—	—	—	—
300+	—	—	—	—	—	—	—	—	—	—	—	—
Uneven aged:												
<100	28	165	720	165	534	1,580	106	380	1,140	299	1,080	3,441
100+	21	77	251	64	407	1,745	22	62	188	107	546	2,184
Nonstocked[e]	—	—	—	8	—	—	17	18	58	26	18	58
Total, all ages	179	900	3,869	1,736	4,625	14,465	759	2,014	6,090	2,673	7,538	24,423

— = less than 500 acres, 500,000 cubic feet, or 500,000 board feet found.

[a] Totals may be off because of rounding; data subject to sampling error.
[b] Includes growing-stock trees 5.0 inches in d.b.h. and larger.
[c] Includes softwood sawtimber trees 9.0 inches in d.b.h. and larger, and hardwood trees 11.0 inches in d.b.h. and larger.
[d] Scr bner rule.
[e] Nonstocked areas are less than 10 percent stocked with live trees.

Table 25a—Estimated gross annual growth, average annual mortality, and average annual removals of growing-stock on nonfederal timberland, by species and owner class, western Oregon, January 1, 1997[a][b]

Thousand cubic feet

Species	Other public — Current gross annual growth	Other public — Avg. annual mortality	Other public — Avg. annual removals	Forestry industry — Current gross annual growth	Forestry industry — Avg. annual mortality	Forestry industry — Avg. annual removals	Other private — Current gross annual growth	Other private — Avg. annual mortality	Other private — Avg. annual removals	All owners — Current gross annual growth	All owners — Avg. annual mortality	All owners — Avg. annual removals
Softwood:												
Douglas-fir	104,041	9,659	28,415	411,698	27,041	253,027	115,716	11,087	86,040	631,455	47,787	367,482
Grand fir	1,669	267	—	13,509	1,907	12,374	7,377	1,341	2,734	22,556	3,514	15,108
Incense-cedar	129	72	—	2,929	541	715	2,173	495	580	5,231	1,108	1,295
Jeffrey pine	—	—	—	41	18	—	39	1	—	80	18	—
Knobcone pine	—	—	—	34	3	—	—	—	—	34	3	—
Lodgepole pine	—	—	—	—	—	—	665	160	—	665	160	—
Mountain hemlock	1,374	66	—	2,754	—	207	—	—	—	4,128	—	207
Noble fir	—	—	—	—	244	139	—	—	—	—	311	139
Ponderosa pine	115	48	—	1,526	292	2,391	4,261	626	912	5,902	965	3,302
Port-Orford-cedar	63	46	—	1,324	147	1,707	505	121	—	1,892	314	1,707
Redwood	—	—	—	872	234	2,792	247	18	—	1,120	252	2,792
Sitka spruce	2,991	609	1,619	17,537	2,726	22,594	4,447	740	3,356	24,975	4,074	27,568
Sugar pine	252	15	—	725	132	5,409	251	50	—	1,228	196	5,409
Western hemlock	19,494	2,526	8,026	98,674	10,703	91,047	5,562	787	22,841	123,730	14,016	121,914
Western redcedar	1,017	238	—	6,103	1,075	16,928	4,868	1,036	2,590	11,987	2,348	19,518
Western white pine	—	—	—	—	—	—	30	4	—	30	4	—
White fir	201	96	—	3,414	422	5,415	482	190	2,951	4,097	709	8,366
Total	131,346	13,641	38,060	561,140	45,484	414,885	146,623	16,656	122,003	839,110	75,781	574,948
Hardwood:												
Bigleaf maple	2,299	695	1,342	9,656	2,492	12,100	10,103	2,448	2,834	22,058	5,635	16,277
Black cottonwood	115	16	—	427	68	—	515	104	—	1,056	189	—
California black oak	80	99	—	427	228	635	2,696	1,174	425	3,203	1,502	1,059
California-laurel	221	27	—	1,655	239	713	282	44	—	2,158	310	713
Canyon live oak	25	13	—	173	72	—	60	29	—	258	113	—
Cherry	102	6	94	484	97	870	458	104	513	1,044	207	1,382
Golden chinkapin	—	—	—	2,980	916	426	169	154	144	3,149	1,070	779
Oregon ash	—	—	—	694	95	100	570	93	112	1,264	187	211
Oregon white oak	179	36	—	1,901	1,311	285	3,710	1,328	765	5,790	2,675	1,049
Pacific madrone	328	317	—	3,742	2,002	3,643	4,769	1,537	2,922	8,839	3,856	6,565
Red alder	25,554	7,262	534	53,659	14,204	41,653	26,988	7,502	8,963	106,201	28,967	51,150
Tanoak	8	3	—	3,941	566	1,802	1,045	152	87	4,993	721	1,889
Total	28,910	8,474	1,437	79,739	22,290	57,635	51,365	14,669	14,296	160,014	45,433	73,368
All species	160,256	22,115	39,497	640,880	67,774	472,520	197,988	31,325	136,299	999,123	121,214	648,316

— = less than 500 cubic feet found.

[a] Totals may be off because of rounding; data subject to sampling error.

[b] Includes growing-stock trees 5.0 inches in d.b.h. and larger.

Table 25b—Estimated gross annual growth, average annual mortality, and average annual removals of growing-stock on nonfederal timberland, by species and owner class, northwest Oregon, January 1, 1997[a,b]

Species	Other public			Forestry industry			Other private			All owners		
	Current gross annual growth	Average annual mortality	Average annual removals	Current gross annual growth	Average annual mortality	Average annual removals	Current gross annual growth	Average annual mortality	Average annual removals	Current gross annual growth	Average annual mortality	Average annual removals
						Thousand cubic feet						
Softwood:												
Douglas-fir	77,679	6,109	13,308	110,897	9,416	82,003	40,350	3,869	23,195	228,925	19,393	117,656
Grand fir	506	237	—	986	122	—	1,117	256	225	2,609	615	225
Mountain hemlock	—	—	—	—	—	207	—	—	—	—	—	207
Noble fir	1,374	66	—	2,311	179	139	—	—	—	3,684	245	139
Ponderosa pine	—	—	—	131	6	—	57	11	—	188	17	—
Sitka spruce	2,352	273	1,619	10,895	1,579	4,043	1,071	111	2,159	14,319	1,964	7,820
Western hemlock	18,470	2,368	7,867	61,391	6,689	33,921	2,891	181	928	82,752	9,237	42,716
Western redcedar	963	233	—	2,414	383	2,624	3,984	847	2,433	7,361	1,463	5,056
Total	101,344	9,285	22,794	189,024	18,374	122,085	49,470	5,275	28,941	339,839	32,934	173,820
Hardwood:												
Bigleaf maple	2,019	636	—	2,467	867	5,548	6,137	1,785	1,885	10,623	3,288	7,434
Black cottonwood	—	—	—	427	68	—	466	96	—	892	165	—
Cherry	102	6	—	118	83	180	405	88	288	624	178	467
Oregon ash	—	—	—	53	6	—	387	64	—	440	70	—
Oregon white oak	8	4	—	202	168	95	2,194	737	419	2,404	909	514
Pacific madrone	14	60	—	—	—	—	—	—	—	14	60	—
Red alder	21,989	6,128	—	20,210	5,899	21,924	13,144	4,091	6,257	55,343	16,117	28,716
Total	24,132	6,834	—	23,475	7,091	27,154	22,732	6,860	8,365	70,339	20,785	35,519
All species	125,476	16,119	22,794	212,500	25,465	149,239	72,202	12,136	37,306	410,178	53,720	209,339

— = less than 500 cubic feet found.

[a] Totals may be off because of rounding; data subject to sampling error.

[b] Includes growing-stock trees 5.0 inches in d.b.h. and larger.

Table 25c—Estimated gross annual growth, average annual mortality, and average annual removals of growing-stock on nonfederal timberland, by species and owner class, west-central Oregon, January 1, 1997[a][b]

Thousand cubic feet

Species	Other public			Forestry industry			Other private			All owners		
	Current gross annual growth	Average annual mortality	Average annual removals	Current gross annual growth	Average annual mortality	Average annual removals	Current gross annual growth	Average annual mortality	Average annual removals	Current gross annual growth	Average annual mortality	Average annual removals
Softwood:												
Douglas-fir	9,857	1,486	12,720	149,133	9,533	65,760	29,503	2,942	28,318	188,493	13,962	106,798
Grand fir	—	—	—	1,847	266	4,441	2,161	525	887	4,008	791	5,328
Incense-cedar	—	—	—	519	85	—	160	49	—	679	134	—
Lodgepole pine	—	—	—	—	—	—	549	141	—	549	141	—
Noble fir	—	—	—	443	66	—	—	—	—	443	66	—
Ponderosa pine	—	—	—	8	16	—	1,157	109	—	1,165	124	—
Sitka spruce	—	—	—	5,585	974	15,368	2,086	512	1,197	7,671	1,487	16,565
Western hemlock	158	19	159	28,858	3,224	28,166	1,612	497	21,913	30,628	3,741	50,238
Western redcedar	—	—	—	1,661	235	8,909	414	94	157	2,075	328	9,066
Western white pine	—	—	—	—	—	—	30	4	—	30	4	—
Total	10,015	1,505	12,879	188,053	14,398	122,784	37,674	4,874	52,472	235,742	20,777	188,135
Hardwood:												
Bigleaf maple	138	34	1,342	4,101	791	4,049	3,130	478	354	7,368	1,303	5,745
Black cottonwood	115	16	—	—	—	—	—	—	—	115	16	—
California black oak	—	—	—	—	—	—	495	297	90	495	297	90
Cherry	—	—	—	222	—	690	53	15	—	275	15	690
Golden chinkapin	—	—	94	1,152	387	163	120	105	—	1,273	492	258
Oregon ash	—	—	—	539	68	—	123	24	—	662	92	—
Oregon white oak	—	—	—	986	396	—	776	210	296	1,762	606	296
Pacific madrone	—	—	—	16	100	398	111	44	95	127	144	492
Red alder	1,587	474	—	12,041	2,909	4,570	7,285	2,107	—	20,913	5,490	4,570
Total	1,839	524	1,436	19,055	4,651	10,237	12,095	3,281	834	32,989	8,456	12,508
All species	11,854	2,029	14,315	207,108	19,050	133,021	49,769	8,154	53,307	268,731	29,233	200,643

— = less than 500 cubic feet found.

[a] Totals may be off because of rounding; data subject to sampling error.

[b] Includes growing-stock trees 5.0 inches in d.b.h. and larger.

Table 25d—Estimated gross annual growth, average annual mortality, and average annual removals of growing-stock on nonfederal timberland, by species and owner class, southwest Oregon, January 1, 1997[a][b]

Species	Other public			Forestry industry			Other private			All owners		
	Current gross annual growth	Average annual mortality	Average annual removals	Current gross annual growth	Average annual mortality	Average annual removals	Current gross annual growth	Average annual mortality	Average annual removals	Current gross annual growth	Average annual mortality	Average annual removals
						Thousand cubic feet						
Softwood:												
Douglas-fir	16,505	2,064	2,387	151,669	8,092	106,115	45,863	4,275	34,526	214,037	14,432	143,029
Grand fir	1,164	30	—	10,676	1,519	7,933	4,099	560	1,621	15,938	2,109	9,554
Incense-cedar	129	72	—	2,410	456	715	2,013	446	580	4,552	974	1,295
Jeffrey pine	—	—	—	41	18	—	39	1	—	80	18	—
Knobcone pine	—	—	—	34	3	—	—	—	—	34	3	—
Lodgepole pine	—	—	—	—	—	—	116	20	—	116	20	—
Ponderosa pine	115	48	—	1,388	270	2,391	3,046	506	912	4,549	824	3,302
Port-Orford-cedar	63	46	—	1,324	147	1,707	505	121	—	1,892	314	1,707
Redwood	—	—	—	872	234	2,792	247	18	—	1,120	252	2,792
Sitka spruce	638	336	—	1,057	172	3,183	1,290	116	—	2,985	624	3,183
Sugar pine	252	15	—	725	132	5,409	251	50	—	1,228	196	5,409
Western hemlock	865	139	—	8,425	790	28,961	1,059	109	—	10,350	1,038	28,961
Western redcedar	54	5	—	2,028	457	5,396	469	95	—	2,551	557	5,396
White fir	201	96	—	3,414	422	5,415	482	190	2,951	4,097	709	8,366
Total	19,987	2,850	2,387	184,063	12,711	170,016	59,479	6,507	40,590	263,529	22,069	212,993
Hardwood:												
Bigleaf maple	142	25	—	3,089	834	2,162	836	185	595	4,067	1,044	2,757
Black cottonwood	—	—	—	—	—	—	50	8	—	50	8	—
California black oak	80	99	—	427	228	546	2,201	877	246	2,708	1,205	793
California-laurel	221	27	—	1,655	239	713	282	44	—	2,158	310	713
Canyon live oak	25	13	—	173	72	—	60	29	—	258	113	—
Cherry	—	—	—	145	14	—	—	—	—	145	14	—
Golden chinkapin	—	—	—	1,827	528	—	49	49	—	1,876	577	—
Oregon ash	—	—	—	103	21	—	59	5	—	162	26	—
Oregon white oak	170	32	—	713	747	100	740	382	112	1,624	1,161	211
Pacific madrone	314	257	—	3,726	1,901	1,609	4,658	1,494	1,525	8,698	3,652	3,134
Red alder	1,978	661	—	21,409	5,396	13,483	6,559	1,304	2,620	29,946	7,361	16,102
Tanoak	8	3	—	3,941	566	1,631	1,045	152	—	4,993	721	1,631
Total	2,939	1,117	—	37,208	10,548	20,245	16,538	4,528	5,097	56,685	16,192	25,342
All species	22,926	3,967	2,387	221,272	23,259	190,261	76,017	11,035	45,687	320,214	38,261	238,335

— = less than 500 cubic feet found.

[a] Totals may be off because of rounding; data subject to sampling error.

[b] Includes growing-stock trees 5.0 inches in d.b.h. and larger.

Table 26a—Estimated gross annual growth, average annual mortality, and average annual removals of sawtimber on nonfederal timberland, by species and owner class, western Oregon, January 1, 1997[a][b]

Thousand board feet, Scribner rule

Species	Other public			Forestry industry			Other private			All owners		
	Current gross annual growth	Average annual mortality	Average annual removals	Current gross annual growth	Average annual mortality	Average annual removals	Current gross annual growth	Average annual mortality	Average annual removals	Current gross annual growth	Average annual mortality	Average annual removals
Softwood:												
Douglas-fir	489,881	38,305	136,416	1,671,631	93,134	1,087,421	480,193	38,706	360,234	2,641,704	170,146	1,584,071
Grand fir	5,854	727	—	56,592	6,587	55,406	27,961	5,048	11,568	90,407	12,361	66,974
Incense-cedar	525	252	—	9,221	1,213	1,275	5,976	802	1,663	15,722	2,267	2,938
Jeffrey pine	—	—	—	115	53	—	191	3	—	306	56	—
Knobcone pine	—	—	—	120	6	—	—	—	—	120	6	—
Lodgepole pine	—	—	—	—	—	—	—	—	—	—	—	—
Mountain hemlock	—	—	—	—	—	805	2,777	396	—	2,777	396	805
Noble fir	5,782	255	—	10,533	994	11,421	—	—	3,582	16,315	1,249	15,003
Ponderosa pine	725	222	—	6,607	1,074	4,640	19,401	2,241	0	26,733	3,536	4,640
Port-Orford-cedar	269	137	—	2,604	279	11,051	1,584	192	0	4,457	609	11,051
Redwood	—	—	—	4,295	927	—	549	23	—	4,844	950	—
Sitka spruce	13,710	1,760	7,315	79,690	10,236	118,091	20,396	2,981	18,764	113,796	14,978	144,170
Sugar pine	1,090	51	—	2,915	519	31,594	1,209	184	0	5,213	753	31,594
Western hemlock	88,103	7,913	37,501	405,044	32,248	394,790	18,288	2,236	86,937	511,435	42,396	519,228
Western redcedar	3,733	809	—	22,727	3,499	63,934	20,445	3,876	8,490	46,905	8,184	72,424
Western white pine	—	—	—	—	—	—	132	14	—	132	14	—
White fir	860	333	—	8,421	874	16,346	2,011	564	10,107	11,292	1,771	26,453
Total	610,533	50,763	181,231	2,280,514	151,643	1,796,774	601,111	57,265	501,345	3,492,158	259,671	2,479,351
Hardwood:												
Bigleaf maple	7,897	1,862	4,618	48,747	6,215	27,902	38,565	8,389	5,357	95,209	16,466	37,876
Black cottonwood	675	77	—	2,568	333	—	2,896	548	—	6,139	957	—
California black oak	136	159	—	1,108	405	254	3,169	1,497	541	4,413	2,061	795
California-laurel	258	37	—	2,335	369	2,334	616	79	—	3,209	485	2,334
Canyon live oak	—	—	—	195	39	—	16	3	—	211	42	—
Cherry	—	—	—	—	—	744	5,585	335	—	5,585	335	744
Golden chinkapin	—	—	—	3,793	614	—	239	112	—	4,032	725	—
Oregon ash	—	—	—	212	17	—	1,344	170	—	1,556	187	—
Oregon white oak	428	78	—	4,121	2,829	468	8,437	1,915	1,380	12,986	4,822	1,848
Pacific madrone	453	509	—	12,450	2,731	6,469	10,395	1,832	5,513	23,297	5,072	11,982
Red alder	90,435	21,631	—	195,383	37,185	150,370	104,661	26,194	31,834	390,480	85,010	182,204
Tanoak	—	—	—	5,754	907	3,689	1,350	208	270	7,104	1,115	3,959
Total	100,282	24,353	4,618	276,666	51,644	192,229	177,273	41,281	44,896	554,221	117,277	241,743
All species	710,815	75,116	185,849	2,557,180	203,286	1,989,003	778,384	98,547	546,241	4,046,379	376,949	2,721,094

— = less than 500 board feet found.

[a] Totals may be off because of rounding; data subject to sampling error.

[b] Includes softwood sawtimber trees 9.0 inches in d.b.h. and larger and hardwood sawtimber trees 11.0 inches in d.b.h. and larger.

Table 26b—Estimated gross annual growth, average annual mortality, and average annual removals of sawtimber on nonfederal timberland, by species and owner class, northwest Oregon, January 1, 1997[a][b]

Thousand board feet, Scribner rule

Species	Other public			Forestry industry			Other private			All owners		
	Current gross annual growth	Average annual mortality	Average annual removals	Current gross annual growth	Average annual mortality	Average annual removals	Current gross annual growth	Average annual mortality	Average annual removals	Current gross annual growth	Average annual mortality	Average annual removals
Softwood:												
Douglas-fir	367,334	22,164	65,087	471,091	35,937	345,538	187,374	15,499	100,248	1,025,799	73,600	510,873
Grand fir	2,466	681	—	4,204	372	—	4,177	997	1,211	10,846	2,050	1,211
Mountain hemlock	5,782	—	—	8,714	—	805	—	—	—	14,497	—	805
Noble fir	—	255	—	—	711	—	—	—	—	—	966	—
Pacific silver fir	—	—	—	—	—	—	—	—	—	—	—	—
Ponderosa pine	—	—	7,315	337	19	17,991	341	53	10,587	678	72	35,892
Sitka spruce	10,883	887	36,469	47,115	5,421	147,405	4,558	483	4,527	62,556	6,790	188,401
Western hemlock	84,801	7,538	—	257,657	19,238	8,719	8,570	670	7,848	351,028	27,446	16,567
Western redcedar	3,513	791	—	9,313	1,139	8,005	17,263	3,298	5,400	30,089	5,229	13,406
Total	474,778	32,316	108,871	798,432	62,836	528,463	222,283	21,000	129,821	1,495,493	116,152	767,155
Hardwood:												
Bigleaf maple	6,748	1,645	—	12,598	2,432	16,754	29,820	6,471	4,531	49,166	10,548	21,285
Black cottonwood	—	—	—	2,568	333	—	2,582	505	—	5,150	838	—
Cherry	—	—	—	—	—	—	5,263	279	—	5,263	279	—
Oregon ash	—	—	—	—	—	—	795	100	—	795	100	—
Oregon white oak	—	—	—	407	298	—	6,440	1,153	821	6,847	1,451	821
Pacific madrone	21	63	—	—	—	—	—	—	—	21	63	—
Red alder	79,267	17,432	—	69,592	14,513	75,227	58,337	15,665	19,893	207,196	47,610	95,120
Total	86,036	19,140	—	85,166	17,577	91,981	103,237	24,173	25,244	274,439	60,889	117,225
All species	560,814	51,456	108,871	883,598	80,413	620,444	325,520	45,172	155,065	1,769,932	177,041	884,380

— = less than 500 board feet found.

[a] Totals may be off because of rounding; data subject to sampling error.

[b] Includes softwood sawtimber trees 9.0 inches in d.b.h. and larger and hardwood sawtimber trees 11.0 inches in d.b.h. and larger.

Table 26c—Estimated gross annual growth, average annual mortality, and average annual removals of sawtimber on nonfederal timberland, by species and owner class, west-central Oregon, January 1, 1997[a][b]

Thousand board feet, Scribner rule

Species	Other public			Forestry industry			Other private			All owners		
	Current gross annual growth	Average annual mortality	Average annual removals	Current gross annual growth	Average annual mortality	Average annual removals	Current gross annual growth	Average annual mortality	Average annual removals	Current gross annual growth	Average annual mortality	Average annual removals
Softwood:												
Douglas-fir	50,526	6,714	63,266	630,321	31,963	276,866	130,509	9,890	117,439	811,355	48,567	457,571
Grand fir	—	—	—	6,323	512	18,219	8,791	2,072	3,032	15,114	2,584	21,251
Incense-cedar	—	—	—	1,869	238	—	378	89	—	2,247	328	—
Lodgepole pine	—	—	—	—	—	—	2,162	315	—	2,162	315	—
Noble fir	—	—	—	1,818	283	—	—	—	—	1,818	283	—
Ponderosa pine	—	—	—	61	49	—	5,664	441	—	5,725	490	—
Sitka spruce	—	—	—	28,163	4,259	83,888	10,298	2,062	8,178	38,462	6,321	92,066
Western hemlock	765	64	1,032	117,288	10,465	113,707	5,354	1,130	82,410	123,408	11,658	197,149
Western redcedar	—	—	—	5,146	667	30,705	1,469	322	641	6,615	989	31,346
Western white pine	—	—	—	—	—	—	132	14	—	132	14	—
Total	51,291	6,778	64,298	790,989	48,437	523,384	164,756	16,335	211,701	1,007,036	71,550	799,383
Hardwood:												
Bigleaf maple	682	146	4,618	21,555	1,857	7,300	6,708	1,406	826	28,944	3,409	12,744
Black cottonwood	675	77	—	—	—	—	—	—	—	675	77	—
California black oak	—	—	—	—	—	—	810	546	190	810	546	190
Cherry	—	—	—	—	—	744	321	56	—	321	56	744
Golden chinkapin	—	—	—	2,459	355	—	112	95	—	2,571	450	—
Oregon ash	—	—	—	128	11	—	480	67	—	608	78	—
Oregon white oak	—	—	—	2,093	906	468	934	350	560	3,027	1,257	1,027
Pacific madrone	—	—	—	152	155	—	101	30	47	253	185	47
Red alder	4,744	1,170	—	45,083	8,285	17,458	27,097	7,104	—	76,924	16,560	17,458
Total	6,100	1,393	4,618	71,469	11,570	25,970	36,564	9,655	1,623	114,133	22,618	32,210
All species	57,391	8,171	68,916	862,458	60,007	549,354	201,320	25,990	213,323	1,121,169	94,168	831,593

— = less than 500 board feet found.

[a] Totals may be off because of rounding; data subject to sampling error.

[b] Includes softwood sawtimber trees 9.0 inches in d.b.h. and larger and hardwood sawtimber trees 11.0 inches in d.b.h. and larger.

Table 26d—Estimated gross annual growth, average annual mortality, and average annual removals of sawtimber on nonfederal timberland, by species and owner class, southwest Oregon, January 1, 1997[a][b]

Thousand board feet, Scribner rule

Species	Other public: Current gross annual growth	Other public: Average annual mortality	Other public: Average annual removals	Forestry industry: Current gross annual growth	Forestry industry: Average annual mortality	Forestry industry: Average annual removals	Other private: Current gross annual growth	Other private: Average annual mortality	Other private: Average annual removals	All owners: Current gross annual growth	All owners: Average annual mortality	All owners: Average annual removals
Softwood:												
Douglas-fir	72,021	9,427	8,063	570,220	25,234	465,017	162,310	13,318	142,547	804,551	47,979	615,627
Grand fir	3,388	45	—	46,066	5,703	37,188	14,993	1,979	7,325	64,447	7,727	44,512
Incense-cedar	525	252	—	7,352	974	1,275	5,598	713	1,663	13,475	1,939	2,938
Jeffrey pine	—	—	—	115	53	—	191	3	—	306	56	—
Knobcone pine	—	—	—	120	6	—	—	—	—	120	6	—
Lodgepole pine	—	—	—	—	—	—	616	81	—	616	81	—
Ponderosa pine	725	222	—	6,209	1,005	11,421	13,396	1,747	3,582	20,330	2,974	15,003
Port-Orford-cedar	269	137	—	2,604	279	4,640	1,584	192	—	4,457	609	4,640
Redwood	—	—	—	4,295	927	11,051	549	23	—	4,844	950	11,051
Sitka spruce	2,828	874	—	4,411	556	16,212	5,539	437	—	12,778	1,867	16,212
Sugar pine	1,090	51	—	2,915	519	31,594	1,209	184	—	5,213	753	31,594
Western hemlock	2,537	311	—	30,098	2,545	133,678	4,364	436	—	36,999	3,292	133,678
Western redcedar	220	17	—	8,268	1,693	24,510	1,713	256	—	10,201	1,966	24,510
White fir	860	333	—	8,421	874	16,346	2,011	564	10,107	11,292	1,771	26,453
Total	84,464	11,670	8,063	691,093	40,369	752,932	214,072	19,930	165,224	989,629	71,969	926,219
Hardwood:												
Bigleaf maple	468	72	—	14,594	1,925	3,848	2,037	512	—	17,099	2,509	3,848
Black cottonwood	—	—	—	—	—	—	314	43	—	314	43	—
California black oak	136	159	—	1,108	405	254	2,359	951	351	3,603	1,515	605
California-laurel	258	37	—	2,335	369	2,334	616	79	—	3,209	485	2,334
Canyon live oak	—	—	—	195	39	—	16	3	—	211	42	—
Golden chinkapin	—	—	—	1,334	259	—	127	16	—	1,461	275	—
Oregon ash	—	—	—	84	7	—	69	3	—	153	10	—
Oregon white oak	428	78	—	1,621	1,625	—	1,063	412	—	3,112	2,114	—
Pacific madrone	432	446	—	12,298	2,576	6,469	10,294	1,802	5,467	23,024	4,823	11,936
Red alder	6,424	3,029	—	80,709	14,386	57,685	19,227	3,424	11,941	106,360	20,839	69,626
Tanoak	—	—	—	5,754	907	3,689	1,350	208	270	7,104	1,115	3,959
Total	8,145	3,820	—	120,032	22,497	74,278	37,472	7,453	18,029	165,649	33,770	92,308
All species	92,609	15,489	8,063	811,125	62,866	827,211	251,544	27,384	183,253	1,155,278	105,739	1,018,526

— = less than 500 board feet found.

[a] Totals may be off because of rounding; data subject to sampling error.

[b] Includes softwood sawtimber trees 9.0 inches in d.b.h. and larger and hardwood sawtimber trees 11.0 inches in d.b.h. and larger.

Table 27a—Estimated changes in area of nonfederal timberland, by owner class, western Oregon, 1986-87, 1997[ab]

Description of change	Other public	Forest industry	Other private	All owners
	Thousand acres			
Timberland area published in 1986-87	862	4,047	1,869	6,778
New estimate of timberland area for 1986-87, based on remeasured plot only	775	3,998	1,854	6,627
Adjustments to 1986-87 area:				
Updates to owner or land class[c]	28	31	125	184
Adjusted timberland area for 1986-87	803	4,029	1,979	6,811
Area change (1986-87,1997) due to:				
Changes in land class—				
Timberland to rights-of-way	-16	-47	-26	-89
Timberland to urban	—	-9	-25	-34
Timberland to agriculture	—	—	-22	-22
Timberland to other nonforest	-7	-8	-28	-44
Nonforest to timberland	—	14	84	98
Other forest to timberland	9	8	23	40
Net change	-14	-42	6	-51
Changes in ownership—				
From other public	-22	22	—	—
From forest industry	18	-92	74	—
From other private	27	237	-264	—
Net change	23	167	-190	—
Timberland area in 1997, based on remeasured plots only	812	4,153	1,794	6,760
Timberland area in 1997, based on all sampled plots	850	4,179	1,880	6,909

— = less than 500 acres found.

[a] Totals may be off because of rounding; data subject to sampling error.

[b] Negative values are losses of timberland, and positive values are gains of timberland.

[c] The classification of owner or land class assigned to a plot in 1986-87 was verified in the 1997 inventory. In some cases, updates were made to the 1986-87 data.

Table 27b—Estimated changes in area of nonfederal timberland, by owner class, northwest Oregon, 1986, 1997[a][b]

Description of change	Other public	Forest industry	Other private	All owners
	Thousand acres			
Timberland area published in 1986	590	1,134	643	2,367
New estimate of timberland area for 1986, based on remeasured plot only	550	1,023	668	2,242
Adjustments to 1986 area:				
Updates to owner or land class[c]	8	15	62	85
Adjusted timberland area for 1986	558	1,038	730	2,327
Area change (1986-97) due to:				
Changes in land class—				
Timberland to rights-of-way	-5	-14	-7	-27
Timberland to urban	—	—	-8	-8
Timberland to agriculture	—	—	-15	-15
Timberland to other nonforest	-7	—	-8	-15
Nonforest to timberland	—	—	38	38
Other forest to timberland	9	—	6	15
Net change	-3	-14	6	-11
Changes in ownership—				
From other public	-7	7	—	—
From forest industry	9	-19	10	—
From other private	—	82	-82	—
Net change	2	70	-72	—
Timberland area in 1997, based on remeasured plots only	558	1,095	664	2,317
Timberland area in 1997, based on all sampled plots	574	1,104	691	2,368

— = less than 500 acres found.

[a] Totals may be off because of rounding; data subject to sampling error.

[b] Negative values are losses of timberland, and positive values are gains of timberland.

[c] The classification of owner or land class assigned to a plot in 1986 was verified in the 1997 inventory. In some cases, updates were made to the 1986 data.

Table 27c—Estimated changes in area of nonfederal timberland, by owner class, west-central Oregon, 1987, 1997[a][b]

Description of change	Other public	Forest industry	Other private	All owners
	Thousand acres			
Timberland area published in 1987	109	1,270	449	1,828
New estimate of timberland area for 1987 based on remeasured plot only	72	1,289	485	1,847
Adjustments to 1987 area: Updates to owner or land class[c]	20	8	6	34
Adjusted timberland area for 1987	92	1,297	491	1,881
Area change (1987-97) due to: Changes in land class—				
Timberland to rights-of-way	-12	-19	-14	-45
Timberland to urban	—	—	-8	-8
Timberland to agriculture	—	—	—	—
Nonforest to timberland	—	—	12	12
Other forest to timberland	—	—	—	8
Net change	-12	-19	-10	-41
Changes in ownership—				
From other public	-5	5	—	—
From forest industry	9	-30	21	—
From other private	9	88	-97	—
Net change	13	63	-76	—
Timberland area in 1997, based on remeasured plots only	93	1,340	406	1,839
Timberland area in 1997, based on all sampled plots	97	1,339	430	1,867

— = less than 500 acres found.

[a] Totals may be off because of rounding; data subject to sampling error.

[b] Negative values are losses of timberland and positive values are gains of timberland.

[c] The classification of owner or land class assigned to a plot in 1987 was verified in the 1997 inventory. In some cases, updates were made to the 1987 data.

Table 27d—Estimated changes in area of nonfederal timberland, by owner class, southwest Oregon, 1986, 1997[a][b]

Description of change	Other public	Forest industry	Other private	All owners
		Thousand acres		
Timberland area published in 1986	163	1,643	777	2,583
New estimate of timberland area for 1986 based on remeasured plot only	152	1,686	700	2,538
Adjustments to 1986 area: Updates to owner or land class[c]	—	7	57	64
Adjusted timberland area for 1986	152	1,693	757	2,602
Area change (1986-97) due to: Changes in land class—				
Timberland to rights-of-way	—	-13	-5	-18
Timberland to urban	—	-9	-9	-18
Timberland to agriculture	—	—	-7	-7
Timberland to other nonforest	—	-8	-21	-29
Nonforest to timberland	—	14	34	48
Other forest to timberland	—	8	16	24
Net change	—	-8	8	0
Changes in ownership—				
From other public	-9	9	—	—
From forest industry	—	-43	43	—
From other private	18	67	-85	—
Net change	9	33	-42	—
Timberland area in 1997, based on remeasured plots only	161	1,718	723	2,602
Timberland area in 1997, based on all sampled plots	179	1,736	759	2,809

— = less than 500 acres found.

[a] Totals may be off because of rounding; data subject to sampling error.

[b] Negative values are losses of timberland, and positive values are gains of timberland.

[c] The classification of owner or land class assigned to a plot in 1986 was verified in the 1997 inventory. In some cases, updates were made to the 1986 data.

Table 28a—Estimated changes in net volume of growing-stock on nonfederal timberland, by species group and owner class, western Oregon, 1986-87, 1997[a][b]

Description	Softwood species				Hardwood species			
	Other public	Forest industry	Other private	All owners	Other public	Forest industry	Other private	All owners
	Million cubic feet							
Volume published in 1986-87	2,864	9,300	3,456	15,619	610	2,047	1,752	4,408
Estimate of 1986-87 volume, Based on remeasured plots only	2,977	10,091	3,988	17,056	511	1,747	1,395	3,650
Volume changes due to:								
Changes in land class[c]—								
Nonforest to timberland	19	54	243	316	9	5	61	75
Other forest to timberland	14	8	51	73	25	11	50	86
Timberland to nonforest	-139	-165	-151	-455	—	—	-6	-6
Timberland to other forest	—	-3	-8	-11	—	-3	—	—
Net change	-106	-106	134	-78	34	16	105	155
Changes in owner—								
From other public	-166	166	—	—	-23	23	—	—
From forest industry	32	-171	139	—	10	-80	70	—
From other private	103	617	-720	—	19	202	-221	—
Net change	-31	612	-581	—	6	145	-151	—
Growth, mortality, and harvest—								
Periodic gross growth	1,297	6,129	1,542	8,969	264	906	470	1,641
Periodic mortality	-76	-191	-50	-317	-42	-115	-43	-200
Periodic removals	-444	-4,750	-1,347	-6,542	-24	-688	-173	-885
Net change	777	1,188	145	2,110	198	103	254	555
Total volume in 1997, based on remeasured plots only	3,615	11,785	3,687	19,088	748	2,009	1,603	4,360
Total volume in 1997, based on all sample plots	3,683	11,483	4,017	19,183	703	2,038	1,591	4,332

— = less than 500,000 cubic feet found.

[a] Totals may be off because of rounding; data subject to sampling error.

[b] Negative values are losses of timberland, and positive values are gains of timberland.

[c] The classification of owner or land class assigned to a plot in 1986-87 was verified in the 1997 inventory. In some cases, updates were made to the 1986-87 data.

Table 28b—Estimated changes in net volume of growing-stock on nonfederal timberland, by species group and owner class, northwest Oregon, 1986, 1997[a][b]

Description	Softwood species				Hardwood species			
	Other public	Forest industry	Other private	All owners	Other public	Forest industry	Other private	All owners
	Million cubic feet							
Volume published in 1986	1,679	2,924	1,269	5,871	411	647	803	1,861
Estimate of 1986 volume, based on remeasured plots only	1,811	3,378	1,330	6,519	350	561	674	1,585
Volume changes due to:								
Changes in land class[c]—								
Nonforest to timberland	6	11	117	135	1	5	14	20
Other forest to timberland	14	—	48	62	25	—	25	50
Timberland to nonforest	-34	-88	-54	-176	-4	—	-48	-52
Net change	-14	-77	111	21	22	5	-9	18
Changes in owner—								
From other public	-63	63	—	—	-23	23	—	—
From forest industry	21	-32	11	—	—	-15	15	—
From other private	—	138	-138	—	—	77	-77	—
Net change	-42	169	-127	—	-23	85	-62	—
Growth, mortality, and harvest—								
Periodic gross growth	1,001	2,094	499	3,594	222	267	219	708
Periodic mortality	-42	-76	-19	-137	-26	-26	-16	-69
Periodic removals	-270	-1,437	-320	-2,028	-6	-307	-92	-405
Net change	689	581	160	1,429	190	-66	111	234
Total volume in 1997, based on remeasured plots only	2,444	4,051	1,474	7,969	561	562	714	1,838
Total volume in 1997 based on all sample plots	2,538	3,987	1,463	7,988	537	527	731	1,795

— = less than 500,000 cubic feet found.
[a] Totals may be off because of rounding; data subject to sampling error.
[b] Negative values are losses of timberland, and positive values are gains of timberland.
[c] The classification of owner or land class assigned to a plot in 1986 was verified in the 1997 inventory. In some cases, updates were made to the 1986 data.

Table 28c—Estimated changes in net volume of growing-stock on nonfederal timberland, by species group and owner class, west-central Oregon, 1987, 1997[ab]

Description	Softwood species				Hardwood species			
	Other public	Forest industry	Other private	All owners	Other public	Forest industry	Other private	All owners
	Million cubic feet							
Volume published in 1987	634	2,976	983	4,592	76	511	444	1,031
Estimate of 1987 volume, based on remeasured plots only	572	3,189	1,265	5,025	36	404	419	860
Volume changes due to:								
Changes in land class[c]—								
Nonforest to timberland	12	32	21	65	8	—	20	28
Timberland to nonforest	-105	-45	-31	-180	-3	-40	-34	-78
Net change	-93	-13	-10	-115	5	-40	-14	-50
Changes in owner—								
From other public	-101	101	—	—	—	—	—	—
From forest industry	11	-49	38	—	10	-10	—	—
From other private	72	265	-337	—	6	92	-98	—
Net change	-18	317	-299	—	16	82	-98	—
Growth, mortality, and harvest—								
Periodic gross growth	87	1,949	415	2,450	17	199	106	322
Periodic mortality	-22	-57	-3	-81	—	-33	-7	-40
Periodic removals	-143	-1,311	-560	-2,014	-18	-111	-9	-138
Net change	-78	581	-148	355	-1	55	90	144
Total volume in 1997, based on remeasured plots only	384	4,074	807	5,265	56	502	396	953
Total volume in 1997, based on all sample plots	363	3,902	1,048	5,313	48	481	352	881

— = less than 500,000 cubic feet found.

[a] Totals may be off because of rounding; data subject to sampling error.

[b] Negative values are losses of timberland, and positive values are gains of timberland.

[c] The classification of owner or land class assigned to a plot in 1987 was verified in the 1997 inventory. In some cases, updates were made to the 1987 data.

Table 28d—Estimated changes in net volume of growing-stock on nonfederal timberland, by species group and owner class, southwest Oregon, 1986, 1997[a,b]

Description	Softwood species				Hardwood species			
	Other public	Forest industry	Other private	All owners	Other public	Forest industry	Other private	All owners
	Million cubic feet							
Volume published in 1986	551	3,400	1,204	5,156	123	889	505	1,516
Estimate of 1986 volume, based on remeasured plots only	592	3,525	1,394	5,511	131	840	413	1,384
Volume changes due to: Changes in land class[c]—								
Nonforest to timberland	—	12	105	116	—	—	27	27
Other forest to timberland	—	8	3	11	—	11	25	36
Timberland to nonforest	—	-28	-66	-94	—	-18	-28	-46
Timberland to other forest	—	-8	-8	-16	—	-3	-6	-9
Net change	—	-16	34	17	—	-10	18	8
Changes in owner—								
From other public	-2	2	—	—	—	-23	23	—
From forest industry	—	-91	91	—	—	-55	55	—
From other private	31	214	-245	—	13	33	-46	—
Net change	29	125	-154	—	13	-45	32	—
Growth, mortality, and harvest—								
Periodic gross growth	210	2,087	629	2,925	26	440	145	610
Periodic mortality	-12	-58	-28	-98	-15	-56	-19	-91
Periodic removals	-31	-2,002	-468	-2,500	—	-270	-72	-342
Net change	167	27	133	327	11	114	54	177
Total volume in 1997, based on remeasured plots only	787	3,661	1,406	5,854	131	944	493	1,569
Total volume in 1997, based on all sample plots	783	3,594	1,505	5,882	117	1,031	508	1,657

— = less than 500,000 cubic feet found.
[a] Totals may be off because of rounding; data subject to sampling error.
[b] Negative values are losses of timberland, and positive values are gains of timberland.
[c] The classification of owner or land class assigned to a plot in 1986 was verified in the 1997 inventory. In some cases, updates were made to the 1986 data.

Table 29a—Estimated changes in net volume of sawtimber on nonfederal timberland, by species group and owner class, western Oregon, 1986-87, 1997[ab]

Description	Softwood species				Hardwood species			
	Other public	Forest industry	Other private	All owners	Other public	Forest industry	Other private	All owners
	Million board feet, Scribner rule							
Volume published in 1986-87	11,786	34,383	12,363	58,531	1,803	5,107	3,888	10,799
Estimate of 1986-87 volume, based on remeasured plots only	12,382	37,339	14,964	64,685	1,567	4,232	3,747	9,546
Volume changes due to:								
Changes in land class[c] —								
Nonforest to timberland	41	137	923	1,101	27	9	163	199
Other forest to timberland	58	15	244	317	36	23	170	229
Timberland to nonforest	-649	-598	-501	-1,748	-23	-180	-247	-450
Timberland to other forest	—	-6	-30	-36	—	-3	—	-3
Net change	-551	-452	636	-366	40	-151	86	-25
Changes in owner—								
From other public	-817	817	—	—	-36	36	—	—
From forest industry	96	-633	537	—	13	-189	176	—
From other private	526	2,656	-3,182	—	33	501	-534	—
Net change	-195	2,840	2,645	—	10	348	-358	—
Growth, mortality, and harvest—								
Periodic gross growth	5,617	23,543	6,496	35,656	951	2,795	1,606	5,352
Periodic mortality	-249	-427	-96	-772	-91	-205	-64	-359
Periodic removals	-2,029	-20,056	-5,395	-27,480	-55	-2,128	-437	-2,621
Net change	3,339	3,060	1,005	7,404	805	462	1,105	2,372
Total volume in 1997, based on remeasured plots only	14,975	42,786	13,960	71,722	2,421	4,891	4,580	11,892
Total volume in 1997, based on all sample plots	15,276	41,679	15,299	72,253	2,223	4,995	4,381	11,599

— = less than 500,000 board feet found.

[a] Totals may be off because of rounding; data subject to sampling error.

[b] Negative values are losses of timberland, and positive values are gains of timberland.

[c] The classification of owner or land class assigned to a plot in 1986-87 was verified in the 1997 inventory. In some cases, updates were made to the 1986-87 data.

Table 29b—Estimated changes in net volume of sawtimber on nonfederal timberland, by species group and owner class, northwest Oregon, 1986, 1997[a][b]

Description	Softwood species				Hardwood species			
	Other public	Forest industry	Other private	All owners	Other public	Forest industry	Other private	All owners
	Million board feet, Scribner rule							
Volume published in 1986	6,337	10,326	4,931	21,594	1,032	1,785	2,119	4,937
Estimate of 1986 volume, based on remeasured plots only	6,889	12,234	5,353	24,476	968	1,484	1,996	4,448
Volume changes due to:								
Changes in land class[c]—								
Nonforest to timberland	20	35	482	537	—	9	14	23
Other forest to timberland	58	—	237	295	36	—	147	183
Timberland to nonforest	-94	-370	-185	-649	-9	—	-49	-58
Timberland to other forest	—	—	—	—	—	—	—	—
Net change	-16	-335	534	183	27	9	112	148
Changes in owner—								
From other public	-266	266	—	—	—	—	—	—
From forest industry	70	-110	40	—	—	-36	36	—
From other private	—	577	-577	—	—	235	-235	—
Net change	-196	733	-537	—	—	199	-199	—
Growth, mortality, and harvest—								
Periodic gross growth	4,286	8,489	2,235	15,010	786	884	885	2,556
Periodic mortality	-92	-167	-47	-305	-43	-12	-36	-91
Periodic removals	-1,226	-5,849	-1,473	-8,443	—	-1,026	-225	-1,251
Net change	2,968	2,473	715	6,262	743	-154	624	1,214
Total volume in 1997, based on remeasured plots only	9,646	15,106	6,170	30,922	1,739	1,538	2,534	5,811
Total volume in 1997, based on all sample plots	10,089	14,968	6,171	31,229	1,692	1,468	2,414	5,574

— = less than 500,000 board feet found.
[a] Totals may be off because of rounding; data subject to sampling error.
[b] Negative values are losses of timberland, and positive values are gains of timberland.
[c] The classification of owner or land class assigned to a plot in 1986 was verified in the 1997 inventory. In some cases, updates were made to the 1986 data.

Table 29c—Estimated changes in net volume of sawtimber on nonfederal timberland, by species group and owner class, west-central Oregon, 1987, 1997[a][b]

Description	Softwood species				Hardwood species			
	Other public	Forest industry	Other private	All owners	Other public	Forest industry	Other private	All owners
	Million board feet, Scribner rule							
Volume published in 1987	3,012	11,079	3,722	17,813	276	1,279	981	2,536
Estimate of 1987 volume, based on remeasured plots only	2,798	11,774	4,966	19,538	126	972	1,112	2,210
Volume changes due to: Changes in land class[c]—								
Nonforest to timberland	21	87	100	208	27	—	88	115
Timberland to nonforest	-555	-164	-111	-832	-15	-121	-154	-290
Net change	-534	-77	-11	-624	12	-121	-66	-175
Changes in owner—								
From other public	-544	544	—	—	—	—	—	—
From forest industry	27	-204	177	—	13	-13	—	—
From other private	399	1,242	-1,641	—	19	223	-242	—
Net change	-118	1,582	-1,464	—	32	210	-242	—
Growth, mortality, and harvest—								
Periodic gross growth	471	7,564	1,852	9,887	48	556	381	985
Periodic mortality	-111	-116	—	-227	—	-86	-14	-100
Periodic removals	-698	-5,419	-2,170	-8,288	-55	-293	-18	-366
Net change	-338	2,029	-318	1,372	-7	177	349	519
Total volume in 1997, based on remeasured plots only	1,808	15,308	3,173	20,289	163	1,238	1,154	2,555
Total volume in 1997, based on all sample plots	1,692	14,545	3,999	20,235	157	1,228	1,007	2,392

— = less than 500,000 board feet found.
[a] Totals may be off because of rounding; data subject to sampling error.
[b] Negative values are losses of timberland, and positive values are gains of timberland.
[c] The classification of owner or land class assigned to a plot in 1987 was verified in the 1997 inventory. In some cases, updates were made to the 1987 data.

Table 29d—Estimated changes in net volume of sawtimber on nonfederal timberland, by species group and owner class, southwest Oregon, 1986, 1997[a][b]

Description	Softwood species				Hardwood species			
	Other public	Forest industry	Other private	All owners	Other public	Forest industry	Other private	All owners
	Million board feet, Scribner rule							
Volume published in 1986	2,437	12,978	3,710	19,124	495	2,043	788	3,326
Estimate of 1986 volume based on remeasured plots only	2,695	13,330	4,643	20,668	475	1,775	638	2,888
Volume changes due to:								
Changes in land class[c]—								
Nonforest to timberland	—	14	341	355	—	—	61	61
Other forest to timberland	—	15	7	22	—	23	23	46
Timberland to nonforest	—	-63	-203	-266	—	-59	-44	-103
Timberland to other forest	—	-6	-30	-36	—	-3	—	-3
Net change	—	-40	115	75	—	-39	40	1
Changes in owner—								
From other public	-7	7	—	—	-36	36	—	—
From forest industry	—	-320	320	—	—	-140	140	—
From other private	127	837	-964	—	14	43	-57	—
Net change	120	524	644	—	-22	-61	83	—
Growth, mortality, and harvest—								
Periodic gross growth	859	7,488	2,408	10,756	102	1,354	340	1,796
Periodic mortality	-47	-144	-49	-240	-48	-106	-14	-168
Periodic removals	-105	-8,788	-1,856	-10,749	—	-809	-194	-1,004
Net change	707	-1,444	503	-233	54	439	132	624
Total volume in 1997, based on remeasured plots only	3,522	12,372	4,617	20,511	505	2,114	891	3,511
Total volume in 1997, based on all sample plots	3,495	12,166	5,129	20,789	374	2,299	961	3,634

— = less than 500,000 board feet found.

[a] Totals may be off because of rounding; data subject to sampling error.

[b] Negative values are losses of timberland, and positive values are gains of timberland.

[c] The classification of owner or land class assigned to a plot in 1986 was verified in the 1997 inventory. In some cases, updates were made to the 1986 data.

Table 30a—Estimated timber harvest volume by year and owner class, western Oregon, 1997

Year	USFS	BLM	Private	Public	Total
			Thousand board feet, Scribner rule		
1962	2,222,200	1,084,495	3,557,388	167,607	7,031,690
1963	2,280,600	1,344,172	3,286,876	208,981	7,120,629
1964	2,366,600	1,614,900	3,469,082	241,998	7,692,580
1965	2,599,500	1,227,995	3,451,309	251,468	7,530,272
1966	2,179,400	1,200,955	3,517,276	221,193	7,118,824
1967	2,046,900	1,064,993	3,364,464	140,259	6,616,616
1968	2,459,074	1,430,983	3,740,345	170,051	7,800,453
1969	2,233,410	1,179,693	3,465,667	214,099	7,092,869
1970	1,814,053	1,013,675	3,212,384	156,778	6,196,890
1971	2,049,449	1,304,362	3,386,347	171,094	6,911,252
1972	2,623,989	1,385,358	3,214,309	257,286	7,480,942
1973	2,598,350	1,454,916	3,050,196	313,586	7,417,048
1974	1,984,502	999,822	2,974,586	230,936	6,189,846
1975	1,509,173	609,454	3,068,680	179,855	5,367,162
1976	1,910,866	1,052,513	2,989,498	220,595	6,173,472
1977	1,788,847	981,535	3,063,233	231,824	6,065,439
1978	2,040,835	812,808	3,064,153	252,314	6,170,110
1979	2,168,621	923,242	2,773,817	247,221	6,112,901
1980	1,562,313	781,453	2,561,131	199,690	5,104,587
1981	1,185,197	662,418	2,225,969	234,277	4,307,861
1982	950,757	299,863	2,850,924	184,197	4,285,741
1983	1,699,479	750,760	2,813,621	272,591	5,536,451
1984	1,879,568	879,704	2,850,422	280,835	5,890,529
1985	2,078,332	875,121	2,938,941	297,838	6,190,232
1986	2,321,819	1,016,923	3,079,296	237,788	6,655,826
1987	2,085,180	1,069,962	2,808,655	239,977	6,203,774
1988	2,237,581	1,398,767	2,778,066	307,711	6,722,125
1989	1,938,334	988,006	3,079,577	226,284	6,232,201
1990	1,012,450	654,249	2,692,540	167,096	4,526,335
1991	999,821	431,595	2,670,437	121,466	4,223,319
1992	617,125	469,987	2,766,905	163,497	4,017,514
1993	416,174	338,713	2,856,275	139,998	3,751,160
1994	256,299	82,980	2,585,910	150,177	3,075,366
1995	197,895	124,655	2,910,499	129,962	3,363,011
1996	189,543	253,967	2,508,241	139,223	3,090,974
1997	203,961	127,305	2,630,328	209,178	3,170,772

Source: Oregon Timber Harvest Report, Oregon Department of Forestry.

Table 30b—Estimated timber harvest volume by year and owner class, northwest Oregon, 1997

Year	USFS	BLM	Private	Public	Total
		Thousand board feet, Scribner rule			
1962	390,900	150,941	593,205	98,180	1,233,226
1963	412,900	123,382	660,941	138,316	1,335,539
1964	422,100	154,902	705,875	123,532	1,406,409
1965	480,100	129,863	754,899	102,707	1,467,569
1966	421,800	154,143	712,167	104,513	1,392,623
1967	375,100	143,530	637,594	74,514	1,230,738
1968	472,784	183,634	855,550	109,425	1,621,393
1969	446,991	121,992	810,336	104,378	1,483,697
1970	360,446	146,307	723,979	65,948	1,296,680
1971	318,842	154,795	848,997	83,576	1,406,210
1972	464,717	176,670	666,540	133,711	1,441,638
1973	494,720	198,424	675,907	172,267	1,541,318
1974	358,458	127,570	617,685	81,617	1,185,330
1975	283,323	53,861	644,605	83,401	1,065,190
1976	361,446	121,695	734,873	123,960	1,341,974
1977	306,621	127,970	662,834	120,577	1,218,002
1978	270,352	88,488	797,421	107,762	1,264,023
1979	394,212	94,543	733,429	139,334	1,361,518
1980	394,749	106,620	576,885	110,079	1,188,333
1981	292,298	102,440	517,775	151,906	1,064,419
1982	196,266	29,294	618,724	89,897	934,181
1983	360,466	105,212	672,437	185,646	1,323,761
1984	426,389	98,300	677,769	195,983	1,398,441
1985	422,075	111,711	742,857	160,313	1,436,956
1986	497,467	109,714	831,087	145,355	1,583,623
1987	364,695	117,999	855,502	134,218	1,472,414
1988	407,889	142,893	880,307	186,547	1,617,636
1989	270,180	123,888	1,003,233	111,663	1,508,964
1990	156,296	72,173	753,843	87,122	1,069,434
1991	210,406	69,918	879,975	73,338	1,233,637
1992	113,020	74,348	941,818	88,955	1,218,141
1993	66,929	49,007	965,834	74,513	1,156,283
1994	34,484	15,765	971,388	109,108	1,130,745
1995	30,013	14,832	1,089,748	102,902	1,237,495
1996	23,373	19,067	926,616	93,762	1,062,818
1997	44,040	16,725	901,271	146,230	1,108,266

Source: Oregon Timber Harvest Report, Oregon Department of Forestry.

Table 30c—Estimated timber harvest volume by year and owner class, west-central Oregon, 1997

Year	USFS	BLM	Private	Public	Total
		Thousand board feet, Scribner rule			
1962	1,126,000	266,583	1,393,768	16,631	2,802,982
1963	1,046,400	398,909	1,292,728	19,535	2,757,572
1964	1,052,500	520,535	1,300,874	25,736	2,899,645
1965	1,229,400	319,528	1,205,070	47,428	2,801,426
1966	993,900	304,721	1,318,737	28,222	2,645,580
1967	884,200	226,602	1,344,033	10,363	2,465,198
1968	1,097,238	311,176	1,413,593	17,641	2,839,648
1969	1,063,764	356,449	1,116,404	26,406	2,563,023
1970	845,337	242,087	1,134,695	24,142	2,246,261
1971	960,677	309,960	1,159,383	16,643	2,446,663
1972	1,189,473	397,117	1,142,425	52,154	2,781,169
1973	1,200,929	395,050	1,209,016	32,632	2,837,627
1974	926,782	291,626	1,054,447	39,502	2,312,357
1975	680,076	159,346	1,182,762	35,069	2,057,253
1976	933,300	243,989	1,110,348	42,138	2,329,775
1977	865,863	247,095	1,021,685	48,487	2,183,130
1978	967,128	286,638	991,032	43,058	2,287,856
1979	1,044,832	239,701	936,352	29,798	2,250,683
1980	732,494	200,386	876,792	37,501	1,847,173
1981	510,394	194,710	772,497	30,382	1,507,983
1982	504,793	138,474	1,072,732	25,376	1,741,375
1983	759,576	193,705	1,037,228	35,168	2,025,677
1984	891,787	237,292	1,060,570	46,550	2,236,199
1985	1,003,342	243,155	1,025,507	42,910	2,314,914
1986	1,005,530	282,627	1,072,671	29,341	2,390,169
1987	1,000,567	292,213	991,357	29,532	2,313,669
1988	1,060,179	357,182	1,029,179	42,166	2,488,706
1989	843,579	243,721	1,103,195	50,670	2,241,165
1990	385,025	185,727	997,735	20,497	1,588,984
1991	431,269	129,965	897,356	21,793	1,480,383
1992	290,348	122,927	958,544	37,530	1,409,349
1993	207,833	62,036	975,049	16,861	1,261,779
1994	116,892	26,140	874,093	20,680	1,037,805
1995	74,137	29,093	939,452	9,039	1,051,721
1996	55,156	64,823	880,002	19,837	1,019,818
1997	51,019	33,188	868,264	20,124	972,595

Source: Oregon Timber Harvest Report, Oregon Department of Forestry.

Table 30d—Estimated timber harvest volume by year and owner class, southwest Oregon, 1997

Year	USFS	BLM	Private	Public	Total
			Thousand board feet, Scribner rule		
1962	705,300	666,971	1,570,415	52,796	2,995,482
1963	821,300	821,881	1,333,207	51,130	3,027,518
1964	892,000	939,463	1,462,333	92,730	3,386,526
1965	890,000	778,604	1,491,340	101,333	3,261,277
1966	763,700	742,091	1,486,372	88,458	3,080,621
1967	787,600	694,861	1,382,837	55,382	2,920,680
1968	889,052	936,173	1,471,202	42,985	3,339,412
1969	722,655	701,252	1,538,927	83,315	3,046,149
1970	608,270	625,281	1,353,710	66,688	2,653,949
1971	769,930	839,607	1,377,967	70,875	3,058,379
1972	969,799	811,571	1,405,344	71,421	3,258,135
1973	902,701	861,442	1,165,273	108,687	3,038,103
1974	699,262	580,626	1,302,454	109,817	2,692,159
1975	545,774	396,247	1,241,313	61,385	2,244,719
1976	616,120	686,829	1,144,277	54,497	2,501,723
1977	616,363	606,470	1,378,714	62,760	2,664,307
1978	803,355	437,682	1,275,700	101,494	2,618,231
1979	729,577	588,998	1,104,036	78,089	2,500,700
1980	435,070	474,447	1,107,454	52,110	2,069,081
1981	382,505	365,268	935,697	51,989	1,735,459
1982	249,698	132,095	1,159,468	68,924	1,610,185
1983	579,437	451,843	1,103,956	51,777	2,187,013
1984	561,392	544,112	1,112,083	38,302	2,255,889
1985	652,915	520,255	1,170,577	94,615	2,438,362
1986	818,822	624,582	1,175,538	63,092	2,682,034
1987	719,918	659,750	961,796	76,227	2,417,691
1988	769,513	898,692	868,580	78,998	2,615,783
1989	824,575	620,397	973,149	63,951	2,482,072
1990	471,129	396,349	940,962	59,477	1,867,917
1991	358,146	231,712	893,106	26,335	1,509,299
1992	213,757	272,712	866,543	37,012	1,390,024
1993	141,412	227,670	915,392	48,624	1,333,098
1994	104,923	41,075	740,429	20,389	906,816
1995	93,745	80,730	881,299	18,021	1,073,795
1996	111,014	170,077	701,623	25,624	1,008,338
1997	108,902	77,392	860,793	42,824	1,089,911

Source: Oregon Timber Harvest Report, Oregon Department of Forestry.